CHESS ILLUSTRATED

CHESS ILLUSTRATED

The Game of Kings

ALASTAIR HORNE

amber
BOOKS

Amber Books Ltd
United House
North Road
London N7 9DP
United Kingdom
www.amberbooks.co.uk
Facebook: amberbooks
YouTube: amberbooksltd
Instagram: amberbooksltd
X(Twitter): @amberbooks

ISBN: 978-1-83886-519-1

Editor: Michael Spilling
Designers: Rick Fawcett and Mark Batley
Picture Research: Terry Forshaw
Illustrations: Patrick Mulrey

Printed in China

TRADITIONAL CHINESE BOOKBINDING

This book has been produced using traditional Chinese bookbinding techniques, using a method that was developed during the Ming Dynasty (1368–1644) and remained in use until the adoption of Western binding techniques in the early 1900s. In traditional Chinese binding, single sheets of paper are printed on one side only, and each sheet is folded in half, with the printed pages on the outside. The book block is then sandwiched between two boards and sewn together through punched holes close to the cut edges of the folded sheets.

Contents

The early commercial photographer Antoine Claudet (right) plays an unknown opponent in a promotional image from around 1845.

INTRODUCTION

THE GAME OF KINGS

For almost 15 centuries, chess has been one of the world's most popular pastimes, fascinating players all over the world. Over the next five chapters, we'll get to know the game in all its rich detail, exploring the different pieces that make up a chess set, examining the game's most fundamental moves, and taking a look at some of the most historic – and beautiful – chess sets ever seen. We'll meet 10 of the most remarkable players of all time, from Emanuel Lasker to Magnus Carlsen, and get to know some of their most exciting and important games.

Before that, however, let's begin by taking a journey through the history of chess, from its origins in seventh-century India to its apparent conquest by machines in the form of the supercomputer Deep Blue. Along the way, we'll learn which king had one of his nobles murdered for refusing to allow him to take back a move, and which piece started out as a humble advisor before becoming the most powerful piece on the board. We'll explore how chess has influenced our culture, from *Alice Through the Looking Glass* to *The Queen's Gambit*; which writers and directors were also keen players, and which rapper based an entire album on the game.

Chess is often associated with love, as this image from the 14th-century German 'Codex Manesse' demonstrates.

THE HISTORY OF CHESS

FROM ANCIENT INDIA TO CHESS COMPUTERS

Chaturanga, an Early Form of Chess

The earliest recognizable version of chess was a game played in India in the seventh century AD. It took its name, Chaturanga, from a Sanskrit word meaning 'four divisions', which referred to four of the pieces used to play it – the infantry, cavalry, elephantry, and chariotry; these would go on to become the Pawn, Knight, Bishop, and Rook of modern chess, respectively. Two further pieces made up the set: the King – essentially the same piece as the King today – and the minister, the precursor of the modern Queen.

Chaturanga differed from chess in several ways. The board may have had the same dimensions as our own, comprising 64 squares in eight rows of eight, with the pieces similarly laid out in opposing lines along the back two rows, but it lacked the chequered pattern we are used to. Instead, crosses were placed on 16 squares – the corner squares, if the board were divided into four quarters – in what may well have been a throwback to another game played on the same board. Additionally, the positioning of the pieces wasn't quite the same as today: the Black King started on the square we now know as d8, rather than e8, which was occupied by the Black minister. And though the aim of the game was to capture the opposing King – broadly the same as modern chess, where a

game is won when the opponent cannot prevent their King from being captured – there were also other ways to win. One was to capture all your opponent's pieces, leaving them with just a King – a manoeuvre known as 'baring the King' – but another was to reach a position in which no legal moves were possible; the player unable to make a move – who in the modern game would claim a draw through stalemate – would, in Chaturanga, be declared the winner. Perhaps the most significant differences between Chaturanga and modern chess, though, lie in the ways that some of the pieces moved. The King, cavalry (Knight), and chariotry (Rook) all moved precisely as they do today; so, broadly, did the infantry (Pawn), though without the option of advancing two squares on their initial move, and with some slight variations on what happened when they reached the end of the board. Whereas in modern chess, a player can choose what piece to convert their Pawn to when it reaches the far end of the board, the older game gave them no such options. In most versions, the infantryman automatically became a minister, but in others, it became the type of piece that had originally stood on the square it had reached – so a White infantryman reaching b8 would become a cavalryman, and a Black infantryman reaching h1 would become a chariot. The move of the elephant (Bishop) also varied according to the region and period in which the game was being played: in some, it moved two squares diagonally, with the ability to jump over any piece on the intervening square; in others, it moved two squares horizontally

This game of chess was carved into the ivory back of a 14th-century hand mirror.

Two women play Chaturanga in this 19th-century painting, while another stands by wielding a fly whisk.

This illustration from the Iranian epic poem 'Shahnameh' depicts the young man Buzurjmihr demonstrating the rules of chess to the Indian ambassador.

Xiangqi, or Chinese chess, remains extremely popular in China. Pieces are placed on the lines of the board rather than within the squares.

or vertically, with the same ability to leap over any other piece; in others still, it could only move one square forward or diagonally. The biggest difference of all, however, affected the minister, who was a pitiful shadow of the modern Queen, able only to move a single square diagonally.

From India, Chaturanga reached Persia – now Iran – where it became popular with the nobility. Some of the terms familiar to modern players came from around this period: the term 'check' derives from the Persian word 'Shāh', for King, and the expression 'checkmate' from the phrase 'Shāh Māt', which in Persian means 'the King is helpless' and in later Arabic came to mean 'the King is dead'. After Persia was conquered by the Muslim Rashidun Caliphate in the mid-seventh century, the game became known in Arabic as Shatranj and, over the centuries that followed, was introduced into new territories by traders,

pilgrims, and soldiers. Brought to North Africa, Sicily, and Iberia by the Muslim Empire in the 10th century, it reached eastern Europe through the Slavs, and the continent's western edges via the Vikings. Merchants carried it along the Silk Road to the East, where it combined with pre-existing local games – most notably, Go, which dates from the sixth century BC – to become what is now known as Xiangqi, or Chinese chess. Played along the lines, rather than the squares, of a slightly larger board – nine lines wide and 10 lines long – Xiangqi remains the most popular board game in China.

The Game of Kings

In Europe, chess was as popular with noble families as it had been among the Persians. Kings proved particularly fond of this game in which they held such a central role. The 11th-century English king Cnut may be best known for having placed his throne on the beach and tried to turn the tide – in a bid to teach his courtiers that even a king's powers were limited – but he is also believed by some to have been the first English monarch to play chess. The 13th-century Icelandic historian Snorri Sturluson writes that Cnut was playing the game one Michaelmas Eve against one of his chieftains, Ulf, when he made a mistake that would lose him a Knight. The king attempted to take the move back, but his chieftain lost his temper and knocked the board to the floor, ending the game … and, ultimately, also his life, since Cnut had him killed at church the following day for his insubordination.

One of Cnut's successors as king, William the Conqueror, was a similarly bad-tempered player, reportedly breaking a board over the head of the Prince of France after losing a game, while his son, the future Henry I, later had pieces thrown in his face by the French Dauphin Louis le Gros after the latter had suffered a particularly galling defeat. (Hastings, the site of William's famous victory over King Harold, would, incidentally – almost nine centuries later –

King Cnut and his chieftain Ulf, as imagined by Welsh artist Morris Meredith Williams.

become the site of a famous and long-running chess tournament won by some of the greatest players of all time, including seven world champions. There have been few instances of similarly poor sportsmanship at any of its 98 events thus far.)

Chess's popularity with kings did not prevent it from frequently falling foul of the authorities, however. Religious leaders could be particularly hostile to the game, whether among their ministers or the common people. In 1061, after discovering the Bishop of Florence playing chess, Cardinal Damiani of Ostin not only forbade the clergy from doing so, but also wrote an angry letter to the Pope condemning the game. St Bernard of Clairvaux banned the Knights Templar from playing chess in 1128, and the Bishop of Paris (in 1208) and King Henry III of England (in 1260) are both said to have ordered priests not to play. Rabbi Maimonides considered chess a distraction from more noble pursuits and barred Jews from playing it in 1195, while King Louis IX of France banned the game entirely in 1254 due to concerns over gambling; his edict had little effect, though.

This ivory Queen was carved in the 13th century. It can be found in the Museo di Capodimonte in Italy.

The Game Evolves

Over the next few centuries, the rules of chess and the shapes of its pieces would continue to develop. Pawns had gained the ability to move two squares on their opening move by around

This illumination from the 13th-century Spanish manuscript Cantigas de Santa Maria (The Canticles of Holy Mary) *shows two men playing chess. The depiction of the pieces on the board distinctly resembles chess diagrams as printed today.*

1300, as a means of increasing the pace of the game in its earliest stages. The 'en passant' rule – allowing a Pawn making such a move to be captured as though it had only moved one square – came later; so did 'castling', moving the King towards the corner of the board and the Rook towards the centre in a single move. Towards the end of the 15th century, two major changes in the game took place. The elephant evolved into the Bishop and could now move any number of squares along a diagonal, though it lost its ability to leap over pieces on intervening squares. And most significantly, the minister (or 'counsellor') became the powerful Queen, able to move like both the Rook

and the Bishop. Historians have suggested that the growing power of medieval queens may lie behind the appearance in chess of a piece whose power changed the dynamic of the game considerably: the 12th-century Eleanor of Aquitaine – Queen of France and England as the wife of Louis VII and Henry II, respectively – and the 15th-century Isabella I of Castile – have been proposed as particularly important influences. The huge symbolic significance of the Queen was so pronounced that in some versions of the game, it was not possible to gain a second Queen while the first was still on the board, to avoid the scandal of a King having two Queens at the same time.

This 15th-century image shows courtiers playing chess at the court of King Louis XI of France.

The rules of chess would not be completely standardized until the early 19th century, with stalemate being one of the last areas to become globally consistent. The rule that a player who could not move was the winner still featured in England until around 1800, while in 18th-century Spain, stalemate was considered half a victory, and the player unable to move would claim half the stake in any game played for money. In some versions of chess played in countries such as India, Burma, and Japan into the early

Johannes Zukertort (left) plays Wilhelm Steinitz in the first official world chess championship match in 1886.

1900s, stalemate was illegal and a player who made a move that stalemated their opponent would have to withdraw the move and play another, while in some parts of medieval France, the player unable to move simply missed their turn.

The Global Game

As the rules of chess became more uniform, tournaments and international matches became more common. The first international tournament took place in 1851 in London alongside the Great Exhibition. The Englishman Howard Staunton, one of the strongest players in the world, invited players from Hungary, Russia, Germany, and France to join some of the best British players in a 16-player knock-out tournament. The contest, though strong, was somewhat weakened by the absence of several players: a boycott by the London Chess Club ruled out many top British players, while some of the international invitees arrived too late to take part; one player, Vincent Grimm, was unable to play because he was in exile following his part in the failed Hungarian Revolution of 1848, while another, Pierre Charles Fournier de Saint-Amant, had just been sent to California as a diplomat by the French government. The tournament was won by the Prussian-German Adolf Anderssen, who defeated Staunton himself in the semi-final and the then Liberal MP for Richmond Marmaduke Wyvill in the final.

The London tournament may not have been an official world championship, but Anderssen's victory certainly made a strong case for him being the world's strongest player. That case was strengthened further the following month, when he won a rival competition organized by the London Chess Club. And though he was heavily defeated (8–3) by the young American Paul Morphy in 1858, his opponent's effective retirement from competitive chess the following year, aged only 22, reestablished Anderssen as the world's best active player, a position he confirmed in 1862 with a victory in another strong London tournament. Four years later, however, Anderssen was narrowly defeated (8–6) by the Bohemian-Austrian Wilhelm Steinitz, who came to establish himself as a strong contender for the Prussian-German's unofficial title.

The match between Steinitz and the Polish-born British player Johannes Zukertort, played across three cities of the United States from January to March 1886, is widely regarded as the first official world championship match; Steinitz's victory, by 10 wins to five, with five draws – despite losing four games in a row after a win in the opening game – thus established him as the first official world champion. He would successfully defend his title three years later, defeating the Russian Mikhail Chigorin by 10 wins to six, with the only drawn game being the 17th and last. A second defeat of Chigorin in 1892, this time by 12½ to 10½, followed a victory over the Hungarian Isidor Gunsberg (10½–8½) in 1890–91; Steinitz finally gave up his title in his fifth world championship match in 1894, at the age of 58, when he was defeated 12–7 by the 26-year-old German Emanuel Lasker.

Adolf Anderssen was arguably the world's strongest player for several years in the mid-19th century, before the world championship was officially established.

We will explore the history of the world chess championship from Lasker to the present day in a later chapter, which examines the lives, games, and careers of 10 of the most remarkable players of all time. In the final section of this history of the game, however,

The Soviet politician and former Red Army leader Nikolai Krylenko played a leading role in the development of Soviet chess as secretary of the Soviet Chess Federation.

we will consider two broader phases of the game's exciting history: the Cold War period when chess became a battleground between the East and West, between the Soviet Union on one side and the United States and its allies on the other, and the more recent rise of computers to challenge even the greatest of Grandmasters.

Cold War Games

Russia already had a rich chess history long before its twin revolutions of 1917. Alexander Petrov, Ilya Schumov, and Carl Jaenisch had all been invited to take part in Staunton's London tournament of 1851, though the first pair declined the invitation and Jaenisch then arrived too late to take part. Four decades later, as we have already seen, Mikhail Chigorin would twice challenge Steinitz for the world title, losing both times. After initially dismissing the game as a bourgeois pursuit, the Soviet Union's leaders soon came to see it as an instrument for propaganda. Lenin played – though an etching purportedly depicting him playing a young Adolf Hitler in Vienna in 1909 is perhaps of doubtful authenticity – but it would be Nikolai Krylenko and Alexander Ilyin-Genevsky who would spearhead the game's rise in the Soviet system.

Krylenko was briefly head of the Red Army before becoming chairman of the Supreme Court and then prosecutor general under Stalin; he was also a keen player who became secretary of the Soviet Chess Federation after writing a letter insisting that the game become part of the revolution. Under his guidance, the most gifted players were supported by the state, which organized tournaments in which they could test their strength against international opponents. Ilyin-Genevsky, a strong player who won several tournaments in Leningrad and once defeated world champion José Capablanca, promoted the game both as part of military education, where it could strengthen strategic and tactical awareness, and also among the proletariat. By 1934,

Bobby Fischer's world championship match against Boris Spassky in 1972, pitting an American player against a Soviet at the height of the Cold War, was one of the most dramatic of all time.

there were more than half a million registered chess players within the Soviet Union, and Soviet players – most notably Mikhail Botvinnik – were becoming increasingly a force to be reckoned with at the top levels. When Alexander Alekhine – a Russian who had fled the country in 1921 and had in 1927 been declared an 'enemy of the Soviets' by Krylenko – died in 1946, leaving his world title vacant, three of the five players who would contest the 1948 world championship tournament were Soviets: Botvinnik, Vasily Smyslov, and Paul Keres. The winner, Botvinnik, would be the first of five consecutive Soviet champions, beginning an unbeaten run stretching for 24 years. Neither Krylenko nor Ilyin-Genevsky were alive to see this triumph, however: the former was arrested in 1938 and then, after three days of torture and a

20-minute trial, executed as a traitor to the revolution; the latter died in a German air raid on Leningrad in 1941.

The man who interrupted this unprecedented – and politically invaluable – period of Soviet dominance was an American whose fierce hostility towards his adversaries made him a powerful, but also controversial contender for the West. Bobby Fischer had nothing but contempt for his opponents and the communist system they represented. In 1962, after finishing fourth in the world championship Candidates Tournament, behind a trio of Soviet players, he angrily attacked his opponents, accusing them of colluding to ensure that only their fellow countrymen could challenge for the title. Ten years later, after the system of choosing a challenger was changed to prevent this, Fischer belatedly ended his boycott of the world championship cycle to win his way through to a championship match against Boris Spassky. Now, the American provocatively cast the match as a proxy for the Cold War, describing it as 'a microcosm of the whole world political situation', as 'the free world against the lying, cheating, hypocritical Russians'. Fischer's convincing victory (12½–8½) did not usher in a new era of Western dominance, however. When he refused to defend his title in 1975, it passed instead to the Soviet Anatoly Karpov, and from him – a decade later – to Garry Kasparov, whose grip on the world championship would stretch beyond the collapse of the Soviet Union in 1991.

Rise of the Machines

Kasparov had been world champion for more than a decade, successfully defending his title five times against Karpov, Nigel Short, and Viswanathan Anand, when he took on a new opponent over a pair of six-game matches in 1996 and 1997. In the first, held in Philadelphia, the Russian unexpectedly lost his opening game but recovered to win three of the five remaining games to take the match 4–2. In the rematch, played a year later in New York City, the

result was reversed: after winning the opening game, Kasparov lost the second; three more draws followed before he lost the decisive final game, and with it the match, 3½–2½.

Kasparov's victorious opponent was not, however, one of the many contenders for his world title; it was, in fact, a computer. Deep Blue, a supercomputer purpose-built by IBM for playing chess, was the successor to a computer Kasparov had easily beaten in 1989: Deep Thought, named after the fictional computer from Douglas Adams's series *The Hitchhiker's Guide to the Galaxy*. Between the two matches in 1996 and 1997, Deep Blue's processing speed had been doubled, and that had strengthened the computer's play considerably; however, Kasparov also contributed to his defeat through human fallibility, missing a draw in game two and a win in game five.

For all that Kasparov's poor play had at least partly caused his defeat, the result was nevertheless acclaimed as a decisive moment in the development of computer chess, the culmination of an idea – that a machine might be taught to play chess – that had first captured the imagination way back in the late 18th century. For almost a century, from 1770 to 1854, an (apparent) automaton called the 'Mechanical Turk' had travelled the world playing – and often defeating – human opponents, most notably Benjamin Franklin and Napoleon Bonaparte. Created by the Hungarian inventor Wolfgang von Kempelen to impress the Austrian Empress Maria Theresa, the 'Turk' comprised a life-sized dummy, seated behind a cabinet and dressed in the Ottoman robes that gave the machine its name. At the start of each performance, the automaton's creator – or, after von Kempelen died in 1804, its new owner Johann Maelzel – would open the cabinet to demonstrate the intricate machinery that apparently governed the Turk, before stepping back to allow it to make its first move. Hidden inside the machine, however, was a human operator, who was able to see what happened on the board

Garry Kasparov found Deep Blue one of his toughest opponents, losing a six-game match to the IBM supercomputer 3½–2½ in 1997.

above through a system of metal discs that hung below the pieces' magnetic bases; he could then use a series of levers to manipulate the dummy's arm to make its moves.

For the 'Turk' to work effectively, its owner needed the assistance of expert players willing to sit inside the machine and play anonymously. Though the identities of von Kempelen's partners were never discovered, among Maelzel's collaborators were several well-known European players, including Jacques François Mouret, chess tutor to the future French monarch King Louis Philippe I, and William Lewis, reportedly the first player ever to be referred to as a 'grandmaster'. The automaton toured Europe and the United States alongside first von Kempelen and then Maelzel for several decades, defeating all comers, until the death of Maelzel's final

Invented by Wolfgang von Kempelen, the 'Mechanical Turk' was not in fact an automaton but rather contained a human player concealed inside its cabinet, moving the pieces using magnets and levers.

The United States' Founding Father Benjamin Franklin was a keen chess player and wrote an essay, 'The Morals of Chess', in which he explored the parallels between chess and life.

assistant, William Schlumberger, during a tour of Cuba in February 1838; Maelzel himself died five months later on the journey home. Donated to the Philadelphia Museum around 1840, the machine was destroyed by a fire in 1854.

It would be almost a century before machines truly began to play chess. In 1948, Alan Turing – the man who led wartime efforts to crack the ciphers created by the German Enigma machine – began work on an algorithm that would enable a computer to play. Unable to find a machine that could implement such a complex piece of code, in 1951 Turing printed out the algorithm and used it to play a game manually, working through the code every time it was the 'computer's' turn to move. More than 60 years later, in 2012, the algorithm was finally programmed into a computer for a game against Garry Kasparov as part of the Alan Turing Centenary

Conference. Though the former world champion won in only 16 moves, he agreed that Turing's 'Turochamp' programme was a remarkable achievement.

Over the next half-century, chess computing slowly advanced towards the point where machines could compete at the very highest level. The first programmes that could play the game successfully appeared in 1957, developed separately by programmers in the United States and the Soviet Union; in 1967, a computer beat a human in a tournament for the first time. The World Computer Chess Championship was first held in 1974 and was won by a Soviet computer named Kaissa. (One of Kasparov's predecessors as world champion, Mikhail Botvinnik, worked with computer scientists in the Soviet Union from the 1950s to the 1990s to develop chess computer programmes, but was not involved in this project.) Since Deep Blue's victory over Kasparov, computers have continued to improve at chess while also becoming more commercially accessible. In 2006, a programme called Deep Fritz defeated world champion Vladimir Kramnik 4–2, though – like Kasparov before him – Kramnik contributed to his own downfall with a spectacular blunder in game two that allowed the computer to checkmate him. Three years later, a version of the programme

Alan Turing created an algorithm for playing chess in 1951, but was unable to find a computer advanced enough to implement the code.

running on a smartphone won a tournament for International Masters. Though computers may never 'solve' chess in the way as simpler games such as Connect Four and Othello – finding the perfect strategy to ensure a win or draw from move one – they have already solved certain complex endgame positions and are valuable tools for human players to analyse positions and develop their play.

Chess in Culture

In 2020, the Netflix adaptation of Walter Tevis's 1983 novel *The Queen's Gambit*, starring actress Anya Taylor-Joy as the orphaned prodigy Elizabeth Harmon, prompted a sudden burst of interest in chess across the world. Commentators said they'd not seen a surge of popularity like this since Bobby Fischer challenged for the world championship in 1972. Sales of chess sets rose tenfold, with millions of people signing up to play online themselves or watch others play on platforms like Twitch. The series won 11 Emmy Awards and two Golden Globes and even – perhaps rather oddly – inspired its own tie-in game, combining chess with cards, presumably for anyone who enjoyed the series but didn't fancy playing chess itself.

The Queen's Gambit is, however, only part of the long history of chess in our culture. The game's symbolic aspects – life and death, war by other means, and its multiple pieces, each with their own particular character – have long made it a popular subject for all kinds of media ... or, at the very least, a rich source of metaphors.

One of the earliest films to feature chess was *Le joueur d'échecs* (*The Chess Player* in English), a French silent movie from 1927 involving an inventor who creates a chess-playing automaton, inside which he hides a Polish nobleman. A more metaphysical treatment of the game came three decades later in Ingmar Bergman's *The Seventh Seal* (1957), widely considered to be one of the greatest films of all time. A knight returning to Sweden after the crusades finds the country in the grip of the plague; encountering Death, who has

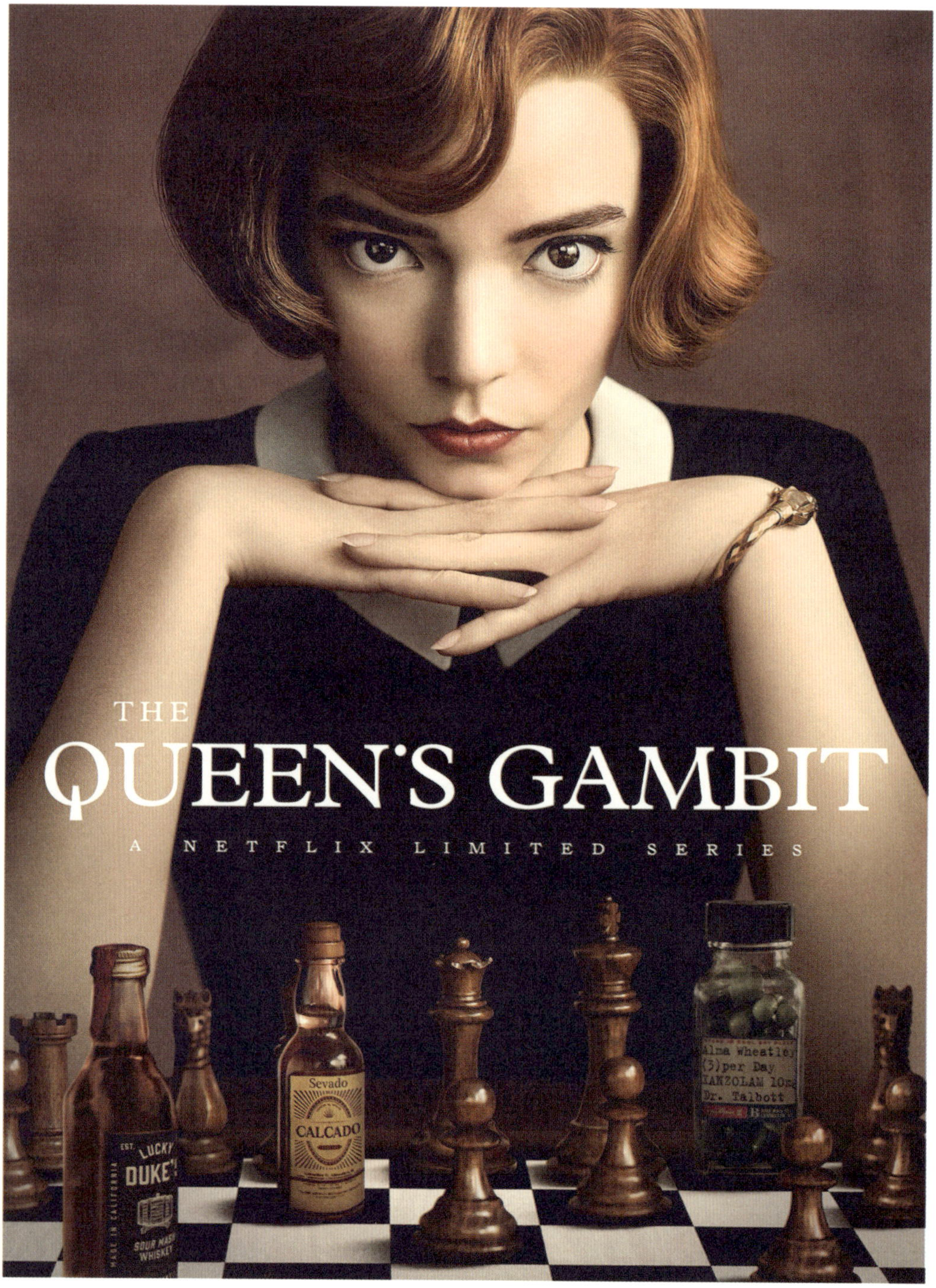

The 2020 Netflix series The Queen's Gambit, *starring Anya Taylor-Joy, suddenly made chess fashionable all over the world.*

come to take his life, the knight challenges him to play a game of chess in a bid to postpone his demise.

Former world champion Bobby Fischer has inspired several films. A 2011 documentary, *Bobby Fischer against the World*, tells the story of his life, from his childhood, through his career as a player, to his later decline. His 1972 world championship match against Boris Spassky is the subject of *Pawn Sacrifice* (2014), while *Searching for Bobby Fischer* (1993) tells the story of another child prodigy, Joshua Waitzkin, whose father's excitement at that match gives the film its title.

A fellow member of Marshall's Chess Club in New York's Greenwich Village, the director Stanley Kubrick was, like Fischer, an obsessive player, earning money in his early years as a director by playing games for cash in New York's Washington Square from noon until midnight. He also used to play on set and chess features in several of his films: most famously in *2001*, when the astronaut Frank Poole plays a game against the ship's computer HAL 9000, but also in *The Killing* – one scene takes place in a chess club – and in his adaptation of the Russian writer Vladimir Nabokov's novel *Lolita*, which features a scene where Humbert Humbert plays chess with Lolita's mother.

Turning from film to fiction, Nabokov himself was another chess obsessive, though he was typically less interested in actually playing the game than he was in composing elaborate chess problems, some of which he published alongside his poems in a book titled – with an uncharacteristic lack of imagination – *Poems and Problems*. His third novel, *The Defence* – also known as *The Luzhin Defence* – features as its central character a Grandmaster named Aleksandr Ivanovich Luzhin, said to have been inspired by the German player Curt von Bardeleben. Nabokov often drew parallels between writing and chess, and in his foreword to the novel's English translation, he draws attention to the plot's resemblance

The Red King and Queen discuss their next move in Alice Through the Looking Glass *by Lewis Carroll.*

to one type of chess puzzle he so enjoyed composing, in which the solver must work backwards to piece together the moves that led to the current position.

The game features in a great many other literary works. In Lewis Carroll's children's novel *Alice Through the Looking Glass*, Alice – once through the mirror – finds herself a Pawn among living chess pieces, meeting Red and White Knights, Kings, and Queens. (As we shall see in the next chapter, Victorian sets typically featured pieces in these colours rather than today's Black and White, the red pieces stained with cochineal.) Crossing the countryside, which is divided – just like a chessboard – into squares of alternating colours, Alice eventually becomes a Queen herself when she reaches the final rank of the board.

In his diaries, Lewis Carroll records beating the sons of poet Alfred Lord Tennyson at chess.

The last work by the acclaimed Austrian writer Stefan Zweig, written shortly before his death in 1942, tells the story of a voyage from New York to Buenos Aires in which the passengers include among their number the world chess champion Mirko Czentovic – an unprepossessing prodigy – and an amateur player, Dr. B, who kept himself sane – or possibly not – during imprisonment by the Nazis by playing chess against himself without a board or pieces. Titled *Schachnovelle* in the original German and either *Chess Story*

or *The Royal Game* in English, the novella has inspired several films, a play, and an opera.

Though not quite an opera, the musical *Chess* is probably the most famous of the game's musical manifestations. Written by Benny Andersson and Björn Ulvaeus – both formerly members of the pop group ABBA – and the lyricist Tim Rice, it is set during the Cold War. It tells the story of a love triangle between a brash American player, inevitably modelled – rather loosely – on Bobby Fischer; his lover and assistant Florence; and a Russian Grandmaster whose story incorporates elements drawn from the lives of both Anatoly Karpov and his world championship rival Viktor Korchnoi. At the beginning of the show, and again at the end, the chorus chant the names of the game's many champions, from Paul Morphy to Anatoly Karpov, but by the time the musical had opened on London's West End in May 1986, their list was already out of date; Garry Kasparov had become the new world champion six months earlier.

Other than this, references to chess in music rarely extend beyond occasional brief mentions of the game and its pieces in songs as varied as Bob Dylan's 'Only a Pawn in their Game', and Taylor Swift's 'Dear John'. Even Chess Records, the legendary rhythm and blues record label, turns out to have taken its name from its founders, brothers Leonard and Phil Chess, rather than the game itself. New York hip-hop collective the Wu-Tang Clan form an honourable exception to this rule, however. Though the 'chessboxing' mentioned in their song 'Da Mystery of Chessboxin'' may originally have been Chinese chess, as featured in the song's inspiration, the 1979 kung-fu movie *The Mystery of Chess Boxing*, founder member GZA is a keen fan of the game, playing regularly against his bandmates. His 2005 album *Grandmasters* includes tracks entitled 'Opening', 'Advanced Pawns', 'Queen's Gambit', and 'Smothered Mate'.

The German Frank Stoldt, known as 'Anti Terror', makes a move against his Croatian opponent Zoran Mijatovic ('the Priest') at the 2006 Chess Boxing Championship held in Cologne.

The timer allows players to keep track of the time each player spends on moves, and ensures neither delays the game.

CHESS SETS

A GUIDE THROUGH THE AGES

Though the rules of chess have remained fairly settled over the past couple of centuries, the shapes of the pieces have proved rather more changeable. In this chapter, you'll discover some of the most stylish sets in history: sets made from woods such as ebony and boxwood, man-made materials like Bakelite and plastic, and even from cow bone, walrus ivory, and sperm-whale teeth. You'll see sets inspired by architecture and by gardens, decorated with flags or patterns evoking grains of corn; some highly abstract designs that bear little resemblance to actual Kings, Queens, Bishops, and Knights; and others where each piece has a face full of character and eyes that seem to communicate intense emotions.

Some of these sets will be highly familiar: most current chess players will have grown up using some version of the Staunton set, which has become the standard set of pieces used by both amateurs and international champions. Others – most strikingly the Lewis chessmen, abandoned more than eight centuries ago on the sands of the Isle of Lewis – may seem strange and unexpected. From that Scottish island, we will journey via Edinburgh and London to France, Germany, and the former Yugoslavia, in search of some of the finest and most historic sets of pieces.

Staunton

The Staunton set is surely the most recognizable chess set of all, as familiar to club and occasional players as it is to Grandmasters and world championship contenders. Designed in 1849 by Nathaniel Cooke, editor of *The Illustrated London News*, the set was named after the famous English player Howard Staunton as a marketing tactic. Author of a regular column on chess for the paper, Staunton endorsed the set, writing about it in his column, and even signed the first 500 sets to guarantee their authenticity. Though sales were initially slow, by the turn of the century the set had become the most popular globally, and they have since become the standard tournament design.

The original sets were manufactured by the games company Jaques of London, whose founder was Cooke's brother-in-law. Pieces were made from ebony (for Black) and boxwood (for White), with lead added to increase stability; felt was applied to the bases to smooth the pieces' movement across the board. Some more expensive early sets were made from ivory; later editions have been made from Bakelite and, most recently, plastic.

The design of the Staunton set is strongly influenced by architecture: most famously, the Knight is said to be inspired by the head of a stallion found on the Elgin Marbles removed from the Parthenon several decades earlier, while the cross at the top of the King and the Bishop's mitre mark the set out as distinctively Christian.

Opposite: This set of Royal Chessmen was manufactured by the British Chess Company, a competitor to Jaques of London founded in 1891.

THE
ROYAL CHESSMEN
BRITISH CHESS COMPY
STROUD (GLOS)

Lewis Chessmen

The Lewis chessmen form part of a hoard of 93 gaming pieces discovered by local farmer Malcolm MacLeod in a sandbank on the west coast of the Scottish Hebridean Isle of Lewis in 1831. Believed to have been made in the late 12th century by Norwegian craftsmen, the pieces are mostly carved from walrus ivory, though a few are made from sperm-whale teeth. They comprise eight Kings, eight Queens, 15 Knights, 16 Bishops, 13 Warders – the pieces we now know as 'Rooks' – and 19 Pawns, suggesting that they made up at least four, and possibly five, chess sets.

Each of the pieces is unique, though they have several elements in common: though the Pawns are abstract shapes resembling boundary markers, all the major pieces are human in appearance, with striking, staring eyes. The Bishops carry crooks and wear mitres; the Knights are men riding undersized horses, while the King and Queen are seated on their thrones. Most interestingly, several of the Warders resemble berserkers – crazed fighters biting their shields ahead of battle – rather than the castle turrets we associate with Rooks today.

The hoard was sold by MacLeod for £30 just months after he discovered them. Of the 79 chessmen, 67 are currently owned by the British Museum, with 11 in the National Scottish Museum; a further piece – a Warder – was discovered in Edinburgh in 2019 and sold for almost three-quarters of a million pounds the following month.

The remarkable facial expressions of the Lewis chessmen – most notably, their eyes – give them a character all of their own.

Northern Upright

Also known as the Edinburgh Upright chess set, the Northern Upright set was popular in Britain from the 1840s to the 1860s and is believed to have been designed by Lord John Hay of the Edinburgh Chess Club, the second oldest chess club in the world. The word 'upright' refers to the height of the pieces, which are all markedly slimmer and taller – and therefore considerably less sturdy – than the Staunton pieces that became popular later, and which are thought to have been partly based on this set. The Queen characteristically has a spherical head without a crown but with an ornamental point known as a 'finial'; the King stands a little taller than the Queen, with an urn-shaped head topped by a finial.

In addition to designing the Northern Upright set of chess pieces, Lord John Hay served as a Member of Parliament and was a rear admiral in the British Navy.

The Northern or Edinburgh Upright chess set preceded the Staunton set and was popular from the 1840s to the 1860s. Both King and Queen bear ornamental points known as 'finials' instead of the traditional crowns found in many other chess sets.

Dubrovnik

Described by former world champion Bobby Fischer as the best set of chess pieces he ever played with, the original Dubrovnik set was designed for and first used at the ninth Olympiad – the world chess championship for national teams – held in 1950 in Dubrovnik, which was then part of Yugoslavia. Only 50 sets were made, and few have survived. The original sets were notable for the absence of any religious imagery, with no cross on the top of the King, or mitre for the Bishop; later variants, such as the Zagreb and Yugoslavia sets, often reinstate the cross and include finials of the opposing colour at the top of the King, Queen, and Bishop. The 1970 Olympiad, held in Siegen in West Germany, used a redesigned version of the set.

Bobby Fischer plays Boris Spassky at the 1970 Olympiad in West Germany, using a lightly redesigned version of the Dubrovnik set from 1950.

One of the most striking features of the Dubrovnik chess set is that the Bishops are each topped with a finial bearing the colour of the opposing side.

English Barleycorn

Popular in the first half of the 19th century, Barleycorn chess sets were typically made from cow bone, with the Black pieces stained red with cochineal and the White left uncoloured. The Barleycorn name derives from the corn grain motif which ornaments the pieces and distinguishes them from similar sets with other types of decoration. The shape of the pieces is defined by the bones from which they are made: the Knights, Pawns, and Bishops are often very slim and stabilized by a wide base; the Kings, Queens, and Rooks are wider, with the Rooks sometimes having a flag at the top. Barleycorn sets were first made around 1820 and were still being manufactured in the 1860s.

Carved from cow bone, English Barleycorn chess pieces were typically coloured red and white rather than the more traditional black and white.

The wide bases of the English Barleycorn pieces were required for balance. Here, from left to right, we see a Queen, Bishop, King, Rook, and Pawn, all decorated with the corn motif that gave the sets their name.

French Regency

The Regency chess set originated in the mid-18th century and remained popular until the end of the 19th, particularly in parts of the world that had been colonized by the French. One striking element of the design is the similarity between the Pawn, Bishop, and Queen, which all typically share the same upper segments, though the Queen – like the King – often has a base shaped more like a vase than the spherical base of the Knight and Rook. In older sets, the Rook often has a similar lower section to the King and Queen, but in later versions the turret often sits directly on the base. The small diameter of these pieces enabled them to be used on smaller boards in places where space was limited.

The pedestal base of the White Rook on square e1 marks this set out as part of an older version of the French Regency design.

In French Regency sets, the Queen (left) and King (right) typically featured a vase-shaped base, while the Knight (centre) had a spherical base, as did the Rook.

Selenus

The Selenus set, popular in Northern Europe, was named after Gustavus Selenus, the pseudonym under which Augustus the Younger, the German Duke of Brunswick-Lüneburg, published his textbook *Chess, or the King's Game* in 1616. The book included illustrations of a range of ornate chess pieces, typically based on flower gardens, and these soon became popularly known as 'Selenus chess sets'. Such sets are typically characterized by the height of the pieces – with Kings and Queens in particular featuring several different segments – and by the elaborate intricacy of their design. Rooks look less like castle turrets and rather resemble the sort of architecture found in parks, while the horses' heads that top the Knights may seem less fearsome than those found in more recent sets.

Augustus the Younger, whose pseudonym Gustavus Selenus gave the Selenus set its name, was the Duke of Brunswick-Lüneburg.

The intricate designs of the Selenus pieces – along with their height – mark them out from other sets of the time. Often inspired by floral gardens, they accordingly became known as Garden Chess Sets.

Lund Pattern

The Lund family manufactured chess sets throughout the 19th century and possibly beyond, with Thomas Lund – previously a maker of knives, pens, and writing desks – establishing the firm in London in the early 1800s and then handing it on to his son William after his death in 1845. William would later be joined in the firm by his own son in the 1870s, and the company continued trading across several sites in the city until at least 1880. Typically made from ivory, with the Black pieces stained red with cochineal, the sets often feature Rooks standing on the same type of pedestal as the other major pieces, and Knights with detailed manes, bulging eyes, and open mouths.

A reproduction of a traditional Lund Pattern chess set awaits the opening move.

Though this reproduction of a traditional Lund Pattern chess set features pieces in black and white rather than the red and white seen in original sets, the design of the pieces themselves otherwise mostly matches those of the originals, including the leaf atop the Queen.

The King and Queen from the famous Lewis chessman set, 12th-century chess pieces discovered on the Isle of Lewis, Scotland.

CHESS PIECES

THEIR ROLES AND MOVEMENTS

At the start of every game, half of a chess board's 64 squares are occupied by pieces: a total of 16 Pawns, four Rooks, four Bishops, and four Knights, plus a King and Queen on each side, line up along the back two ranks of the board. By the end of the game, only a few will be left – perhaps only the two Kings! – as the rest of the pieces are captured and exchanged.

Each chess piece has its own strengths and weaknesses, and these develop as the game advances through the opening, to the middle game, and finally the endgame. Some pieces are stronger when the board is full of pieces and space is at a premium, while others are at their best on the wide empty spaces of a near-empty board.

Playing chess well – whether that's launching a decisive attack on the enemy King, or heroically preventing your opponent's superior forces from breaking through to reach your own King – requires the ability to know those strengths and to use them in combination.

In this chapter, I will introduce each of the pieces that make up a chess set, explaining how they move, how best to use them, and even how some of them got their names.

The King

The most important piece in the entire game is also one of the weakest. It can only move one square at a time in any direction – vertically, horizontally, or diagonally – and must be defended with the utmost care, since losing your King means losing the game. When your King is attacked by another piece, it is said to be 'in check', and you must immediately defend it: either by moving your King, by blocking the attack with another piece, or by capturing the attacking piece. If you can do none of these things, then that is 'checkmate' and the end of the game. (The term 'checkmate' is said to derive from the Arabic expression *shah mat*, 'the King died'.)

In the early stages of the game, the King must be kept safe, often sheltering in the corner of the board behind a wall of Pawns. Though the piece starts the game in the middle of the back row, on square e1 – for White – or e8 – for Black – a special move known as 'castling' enables the King to move towards the safety of the corner and the Rook to move towards the centre of the row. Towards the end of the game, however – in what is known as the 'endgame', when many of the stronger pieces have been captured – the King can become much more powerful, able to roam across the board, capturing enemy Pawns while defending its own, and even helping to checkmate the opposing King by preventing his escape.

The King can move one square at a time in any direction.

The Queen

The Queen is the most powerful piece on the chess board. Like the King, it can move in any direction – vertically, horizontally, and diagonally; unlike the King, however, it can move any number of squares at a time. This makes it easy for the Queen to exert influence all the way across the board from any position, sometimes even threatening multiple opposing pieces on both sides of the board at once, in a manoeuvre known as a 'fork'.

As the most powerful piece, the Queen is also the most valuable – after the King, of course – and players must take care not to expose it to danger: in the opening stage, when the centre of the board is often full of pieces, advancing the Queen too far can easily lead to it getting trapped and captured.

The Queen's great power means that it is rarely exchanged for less valuable pieces, but only for the opposing Queen. An exciting exception to this rule, however, is the Queen sacrifice, when the player allows this most valuable piece to be captured in return for a significant tactical advantage – typically, the chance of an immediate win through checkmate. Queen sacrifices can be some of the most brilliant and thrilling moves in chess.

The Queen begins the game next to her King, on square d1 (for White) or d8 (for Black); this square always matches the colour of the Queen – if the colour does not match, then the board has been set up incorrectly!

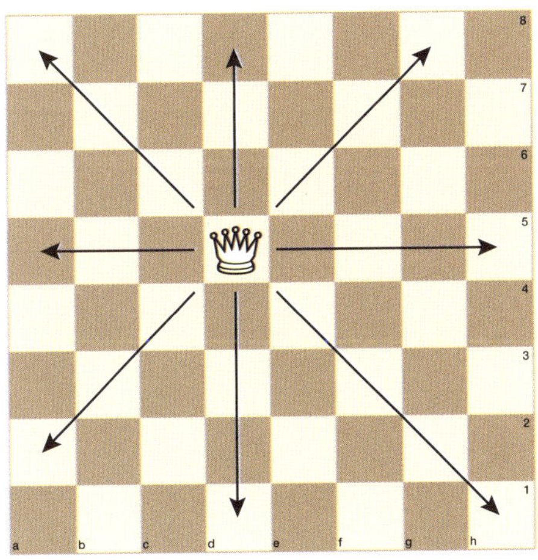

The Queen can move any number of squares at a time, either diagonally or in a straight line.

The Rook

After the Queen, the next most powerful pieces in Chess are the Rooks, which can move any number of squares at a time, either horizontally or vertically. Each player starts with two Rooks, stationed at the very corners of the board, on the squares a1 and h1 for White, and a8 and h8 for Black.

To be most effective, a Rook needs access to an 'open' file, without any Pawns blocking the way; to achieve this, players typically move their Rooks towards the centre of the back rank during the opening, once the other pieces have moved forward, since central Pawns are often the first to be exchanged, opening up the central files.

Rooks become increasingly powerful as the game moves towards the endgame, as pieces are exchanged, and files therefore open up. Advancing your Rook to the seventh rank can be especially effective, since it can attack opposing

Pawns from there while simultaneously threatening the enemy King; placing both your Rooks together on this rank, where they can defend each other, makes them even more dangerous.

The Rook's name comes from a Persian word meaning 'chariot'; the piece's resemblance to a crenellated turret, however, has led to it becoming informally referred to as a 'castle' in English, and as a 'tower' in several European languages including French, German, and Italian. In other languages, it is known as the 'ship' or 'boat', the 'cannon', or even, in certain Indian languages, as the 'elephant'.

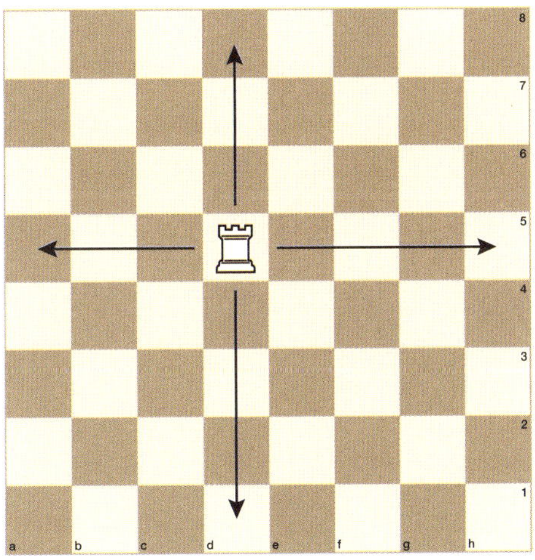

Rooks move in straight lines along the ranks and files of the board.

The Bishop

Each player has two Bishops, which move diagonally, always remaining on squares of the same colour as the square they started on – c1 and f1 for White, and c8 and f8 for Black. As a result, one Bishop on each side moves on the white squares (the 'light-squared Bishop') while the other moves on the black (the 'dark-squared Bishop'). A Bishop is typically regarded as equal in value to a Knight, and less valuable than a Rook or Queen.

Bishops are most powerful when placed in the middle of the board, where they can control as many squares as possible. Two centrally placed Bishops, working together, can effectively control the whole board. If a player has exchanged one of their Bishops, they should try to place their Pawns on squares of the opposite colour to their remaining Bishop – on the black squares if they have a 'light-squared Bishop', for instance – both to ensure that the combination of Pawns and Bishop can control squares of both colours, and to avoid the Bishop being hemmed in by its own Pawns.

Originally, Bishops could only move two squares at a time along diagonals but could jump over pieces placed on intervening squares.

The groove at the top of the piece gave rise to its English name of 'Bishop' because it resembled a bishop's mitre, but in other languages the piece is known as the 'jester' (French and Romanian), the 'archer' (Czech and Slovak), and the 'elephant' (Chinese, Persian, and Turkish).

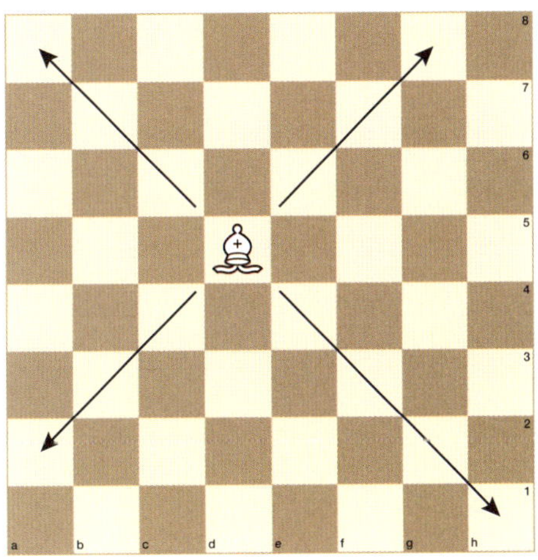

Bishops move along the board's diagonals, any number of squares at a time.

The Knight

The Knight is one of the most unusual and fascinating pieces on the board. Starting on squares b1 and g1 for White, and b8 and g8 for Black, it moves in an L-shape, either two squares horizontally and one square vertically, or two squares vertically and one square horizontally. Uniquely, it can – like the horse it resembles – also jump over any pieces in its way. This method of movement has not changed since the sixth century AD.

Knights are typically regarded as being of approximately equal worth to Bishops, but the two pieces have very different strengths: a Bishop is often at its strongest in an open position, when its movements are not blocked by other pieces, but a Knight is stronger in closed positions, where its ability to jump over pieces can give it an advantage over other, usually more valuable, pieces. And though Knights lack the speed and range of other pieces – it will take a Knight four moves to get from one edge of the board to the other, when pieces like Queens, Bishops, and Rooks can do it in a single move – they are particularly effective at forks, attacking two enemy pieces at once.

In many other languages, the Knight is known as the 'horse', though some – such as German and Danish – call it the 'jumper', on account of its movement. The piece has also given its name to a mathematical problem, The Knight's Tour Problem, which establishes a sequence in which the Knight visits every square of the board only once.

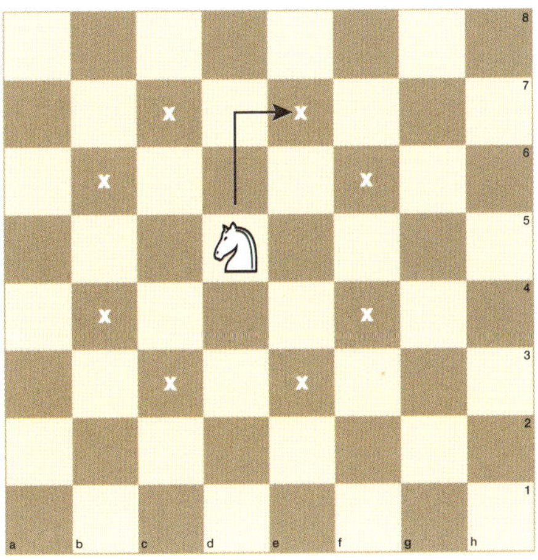

The Knight moves two squares in one direction and one in another; it is the only piece that can always jump over others.

The Pawn

Though Pawns might seem the least important of the pieces on a chess board, their value only increases as the game continues, as Queens, Rooks, Bishops, and Knights are gradually exchanged and captured; towards the end of a game, an extra Pawn can often be the difference between victory and defeat. At the start of the game, eight Pawns line up on each side in a row ahead of the other pieces, on squares a2–h2 for White, and a7–h7 for Black.

Pawns have several unique features that set them apart from other pieces on the board, and these relate to how they move. Though Pawns typically move forward only one square at a time, there are several exceptions to this rule. Firstly, they cannot capture pieces placed directly in front of them but, instead, they capture pieces one square diagonally in front of them, on either side. Secondly, they can, on the very first move, choose to move forward two squares rather than one – but if, in doing so, they move past a square where an opposing Pawn could have captured them (from d2 to d4, when an opposing Pawn stands on e4, for instance), then the opposing Pawn can capture them as if they had only moved one square; this is called capturing 'en passant', meaning 'in passing'.

Finally, and most importantly, a Pawn that moves so far forward that it reaches the final rank of the board can be promoted to another piece – typically, a Queen, though other pieces are allowed.

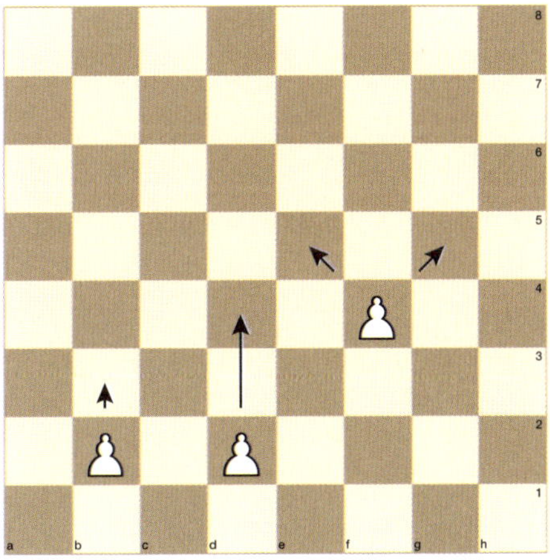

Pawns typically move forwards one square at a time, though they can choose to move two squares forward on their opening move. They capture other pieces diagonally.

World champion Ding Liren prepares to move his Knight.

PLAYING THE GAME

10 BASIC OPENINGS AND MOVES

At the start of any game of chess, the person playing White has a choice of 20 possible opening moves: advancing one of their eight Pawns one square or two, or moving one of their Knights to the left or the right. Their opponent has an identical set of options, meaning that the number of possible positions on the board after one move each is already 400 – 20 multiplied by 20.

As the game continues, this number rapidly becomes mind-bogglingly high. Mathematicians have calculated that there are over nine million possible positions after each player has played their first three moves, and that number soars to more than 318 billion after just one more move on each side. The Shannon Number, named after the American mathematician Claude Shannon, represents the number of possible positions for a typical 40-move game of chess; it is higher than the number of atoms in the known universe.

Thankfully for players, most chess games, particularly in the opening, feature common types of move whose benefits – and sometimes risks – are well known. In this chapter, we will explore 10 key types of move, and why you should consider playing them.

Pawn to e4

Opening the game by advancing your King's Pawn – the Pawn in front of your King – two squares has many benefits. It stakes an immediate hold on the centre of the board, as your Pawn occupies one key central square (e4) and threatens two more squares in your opponent's half of the board, d5 and f5. It also opens up diagonal lines for both your Bishop and your Queen, two pieces that need space to be effective. Almost half of all games begin with e4, and the great Bobby Fischer started with this move in an astonishing 93% of the games he played as White, winning almost two-thirds of those games.

Black can respond in a variety of ways. If they also advance their King's Pawn two spaces, mirroring White's move, then White can reply

Chess notation

The most popular system used today to record chess games is called algebraic notation. Each of the pieces is signified by a letter: K for King, Q for Queen, B for Bishop, N for Knight (since K is already in use for the King), and R for Rook. (No letter is used for Pawns.)

Each pair of moves – one for White and one for Black – is numbered, and the move is written as follows: 32 Re6 means that White's Rook moves to the square e6. If either of White's Rooks could make this move, then the file of the Rook is included in the notation: so, 32 Rde6 means that White's Rook that was on the d-file now moves to e6.

When a move involves a capture, an 'x' is added between the piece and the square it moves to: so, 33 ... Nxf5 means that Black's Knight captures the piece that was on f5.

by moving their Knight to f3 – leading to the Ruy Lopez opening, named after a 16th-century Spanish priest who wrote a study of chess openings. Alternatively, White can advance their f-Pawn two squares in the risky King's Gambit, which offers Black the chance to win a Pawn – and weakens White's King-side defences – in return for exciting attacking opportunities against Black's King.

The most popular response by Black to White's initial move e4, however, is to move their c-Pawn forward two squares to c5. This leads to the Sicilian Defence, an exciting opening in which Black attempts not just to cancel out White's initial advantage but fights to gain an advantage of their own.

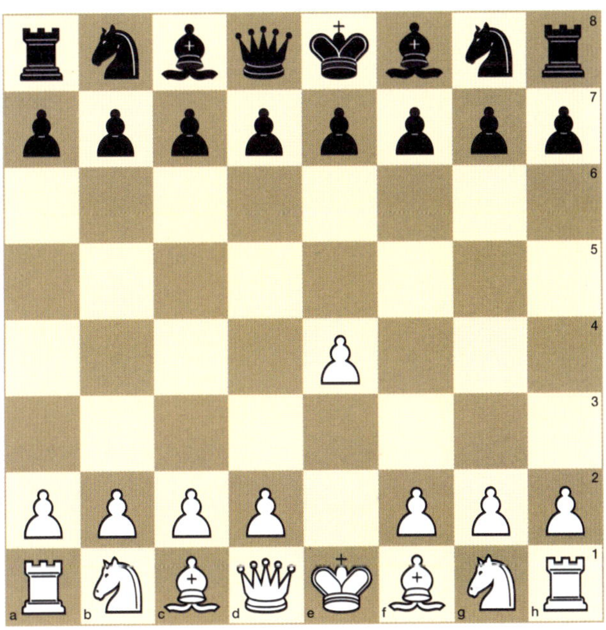

Pawn to d4

Advancing your Queen's Pawn two squares to d4 is the second most popular opening move, accounting for just over a third of all games. It was former world champion Garry Kasparov's favourite opening move, by a small margin from e4, and is particularly popular at the very highest level. Opening with d4 might seem similar to e4 – it too stakes a claim on the centre of the board and opens up a diagonal for a Bishop – but it involves

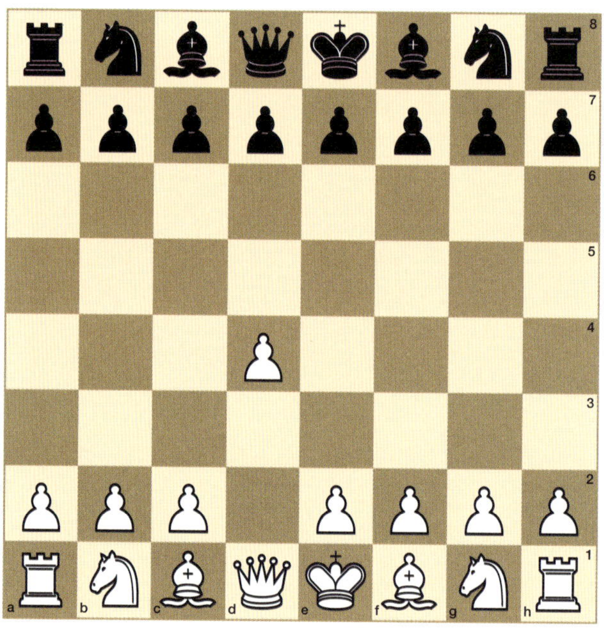

some significant differences. It discourages Black from responding by advancing either their King's Pawn to e5 (where it could be captured) or their Queen's Knight to c6 (where it would be threatened by a further advance from the Queen's Pawn). More popular responses are d5, mirroring White's move, or advancing the King's Knight to f6.

There are a great many Queen's Pawn openings, as games beginning with d4 are known; they often lead to less tactical and more positional games than King's Pawn openings (which begin with e4). If Black responds with d5, then White can advance their Pawn on the c-file – the Queen's Bishop's Pawn – in an opening known as the Queen's Gambit. The most popular response to d4 for Black, though, is to play Knight to f6, after which White usually plays c4, and Black typically responds with either e6 – which can lead to the Nimzo-Indian Defence, the Queen's Indian Defence, or the Bogo-Indian Defence, among many others – or g6, leading to the King's Indian Defence or the Grünfeld Defence.

Pawn to c4

The fourth most popular opening move for White, advancing the c-Pawn two squares, is known as the English Opening, taking its name from the English player Howard Staunton, who first played the move in the mid-19th century. It attacks the key central square d5, opens up options for the Queen to move diagonally, and ensures that if White later wants to move their Queen's Knight to the useful square c3, doing so will not block the c-Pawn behind it.

Black has a wide range of options in response, some of which – if White later plays their d-Pawn forward two squares – can lead to Queen's Pawn openings; this process of reaching a familiar opening from a different order of moves is known as 'transposition'. For instance, if Black moves their Knight to f6 or advances their g-Pawn a single square, this will typically 'transpose' into an Indian Defence; playing 1 … e6, then 2 d4 from White – advancing the Queen's Pawn two squares – may lead to the Queen's Gambit Declined.

However, if Black matches White's opening move by advancing their own c-Pawn two squares – 1 … c5 – then this is called the Symmetrical Defence. Games beginning with this opening typically revolve around each side's attempts to advance their d-Pawn, and White will often play their King's Knight to f3 to support advancing their d-Pawn to d4. Alternatively, advancing the other Knight to c3 – attacking d5 – signals that White may be more concerned with preventing Black's d-Pawn from advancing than with immediately advancing their own.

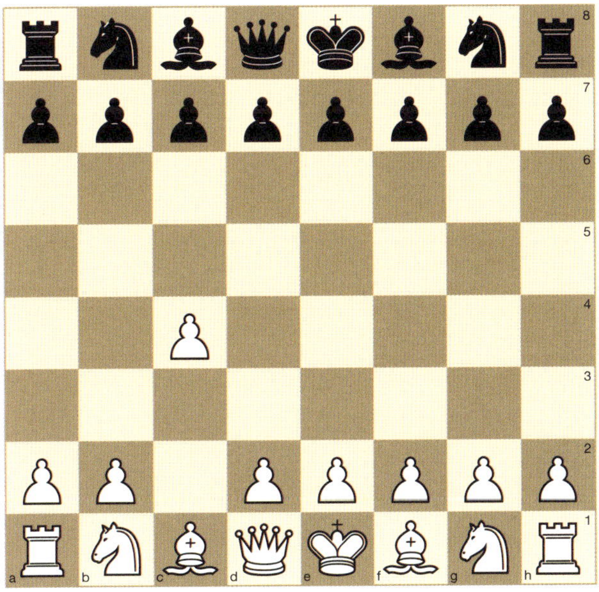

Pawn to d6

Advancing the d-Pawn just a single square, to d6, has several benefits for Black. It opens a diagonal for the Queen's Bishop to advance along, frees up the d7 square for the Queen, and helps Black to establish a defensive foothold in the central files. The move plays a part in several popular openings for Black, including the Sicilian Defence, where Black responds to White's initial 1 e4 with 1 … c5,

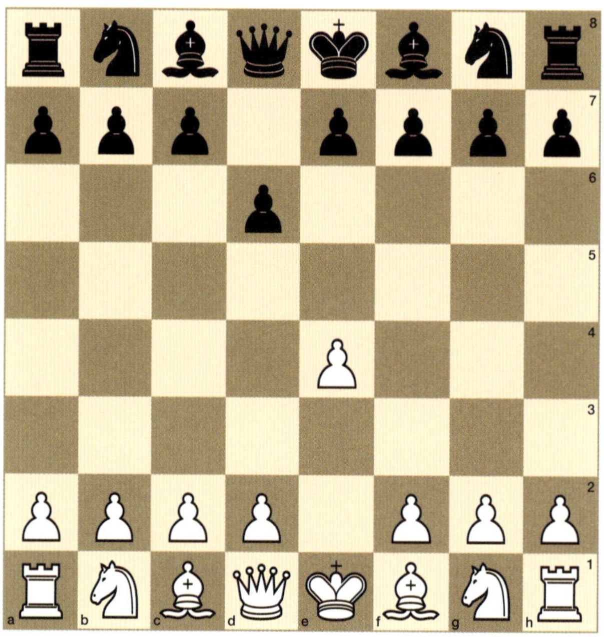

and then replies to White's typical next move, Knight to f3 (Nf3), by playing d6, supporting the c-Pawn.

If Black plays 1 … d6 in response to White's initial 1 e4, then this is the Pirc Defence (pictured), named after the Slovenian Grandmaster Vasja Pirc, who was Yugoslavian champion five times between 1935 and 1953. It is one of the so-called 'hypermodern' openings, in which Black attacks the centre of the board from the flanks rather than attempting to place their own Pawns in key central squares. After 1 e4 d6, White advances their d-Pawn two squares (2 d4), taking advantage of the fact that Black has not laid immediate claim to the centre of the board with a Pawn; Black in turn advances their King's Knight (2 … Nf6).

White then advances the Queen's Knight (3 Nc3) and Black brings forward the King's Knight's Pawn a single square (3 … g6) so that its Bishop can occupy the vacated square on g7 and attack the centre of the board along the long a1–h8 diagonal.

Knight to f3 / c3

The squares c3 and f3 provide excellent bases for White's Knights, particularly in the opening. (The squares c6 and f6 are similarly useful for Black's Knights.) From here, the Knights can threaten – or defend – key squares in the centre of the board, often occupied by Pawns in the early stages of the game: for instance, the White Knight on f3 in the position pictured threatens the Black Pawn on e5, forcing Black to defend it with the Knight on c6; it also defends the vital d4 square ahead of a possible advance to that square of White's d-Pawn. When White has Knights on both c3 and f3, all four of the central squares – d4, e4, d5, and e5 – are covered by the pair.

For these reasons, moving Knights to f3 or c3 – 'developing' the Knight by moving it from its starting place into a more effective position on the board – forms a key part of many openings. Nf3, for instance, features as the second move in both the Ruy Lopez (1 e4 e5 2 Nf3 Nc6), as pictured, and the Sicilian (1 e4 c5 2 Nf3); Nc3 is a common early move in the Queen's Gambit Declined (1 d4 d5 2 c4 Nf6 3 Nc3).

Developing Knights away from the back row of the board also makes it easier to move the King to safety in the corner of the board by castling, which we will come to shortly.

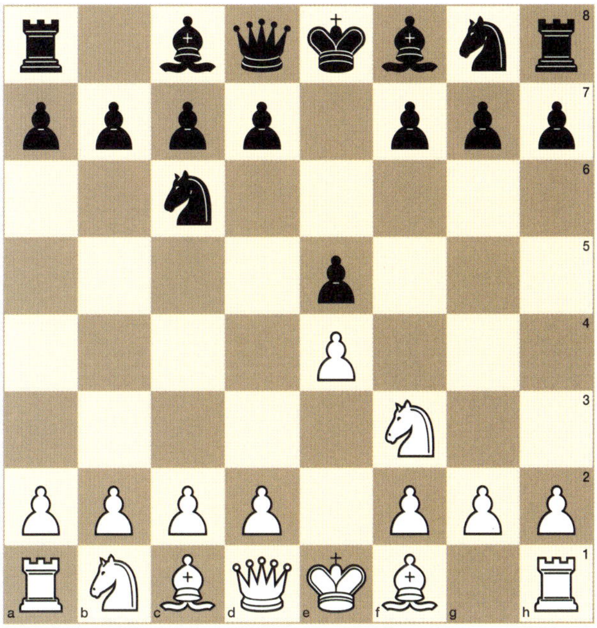

Bishop to c4/f4

Developing your Bishops is an important task in the opening, but it can sometimes be difficult to find the best place for them: leaving them on the back rows of the board can limit their influence, but advancing them too far can leave them vulnerable to attacks, particularly from opposition Pawns, forcing them to retreat or even causing them to be trapped and captured.

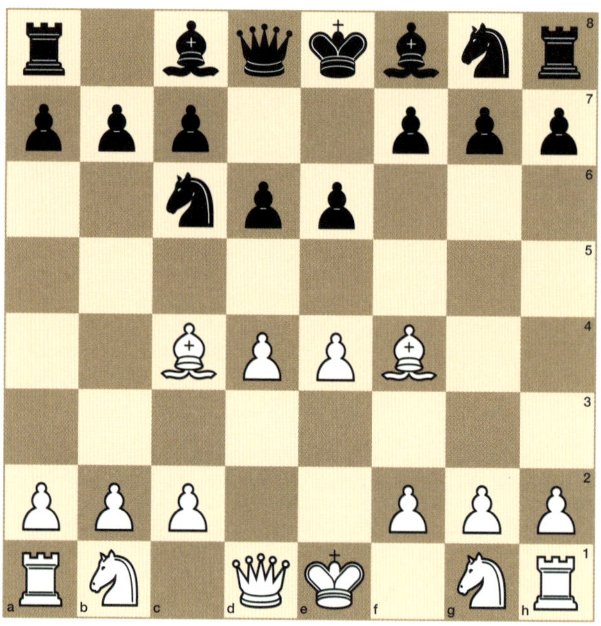

One method of developing your Bishops is to advance your d- and e-Pawns, allowing the Bishops to advance along the f1–a6 and c1–h6 diagonals for White – f8–a3 and c8–h3 for Black – to parts of the board where they can influence the game more strongly. In the Ruy Lopez opening, for instance, the White King's Bishop advances to b5, where it threatens the Black Knight on f6 (1 e4 e5 2 Nf3 Nc6 3 Bb5), but Black then immediately advances the a-Pawn (3 … a7), forcing the Bishop either to retreat to a4 (4 Ba4) or to exchange itself for the opposition Knight (4 Bxc6 dxc6).

Placing the Bishop on c4 (pictured) allows it to exert more influence on the centre of the board – and to attack the f7 square, potentially a weak spot in the Black King's defences until he retreats to the corner of the board. Here too, though, it can be vulnerable to an advancing Pawn – in this case, the Black d-Pawn, if it receives enough support from Black's other pieces. We will consider an alternative option for developing Bishops in the next section.

Bishop to b2/g2

Advancing the Knight's Pawn allows a player to move the Bishop to the square vacated by that Pawn: b2 or g2 for White, and b7 or g7 for Black. This combination of moves has the advantage of placing the Bishop on one of the board's longest diagonals, giving it plenty of options for movement, while also protecting it from attack; it makes good use of the fact that Bishops, unlike Knights, are highly effective over long distances. Additionally, if a player has chosen to place their King on the same side of the board as the Bishop, then that Bishop can help strengthen the King's defences, with the Bishop and Pawns combining to attack – and defend – squares of both colours. Exchanging the Bishop can, however, leave the defences considerably weakened, and should generally be avoided.

This method of developing your Bishop is known as a 'fianchetto', a diminutive version of the Italian word for 'flank'. Fianchettoed Bishops are common in many hypermodern openings, where one side allows the other to occupy the centre of the board while preparing to attack the centre from the safety of the flanks. The picture shows the position after eight moves of a game from 1925 between the Polish player Akiba Rubinstein and the Dane Aron Nimzowitsch, a prominent proponent of hypermodern openings; though all four Bishops have been fianchettoed, the first use of this term to describe the manoeuvre came two years later, in 1927.

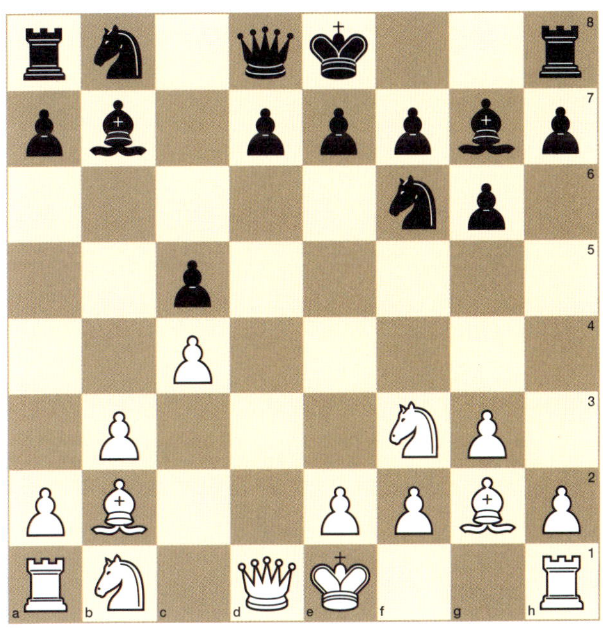

Castling Kingside
(O-O)

Castling is a special type of move for the King and Rook, the only move in chess where one player moves two of their own pieces at once (and the only move in which the King can move more than one square at a time). It can only be performed under certain conditions: if neither King nor Rook has already moved; if there are no pieces on the squares between the King and Rook; and if the King is not already in check and, in making the move, does not pass over or end up on a square where he would be in check.

There are two types of castling, Kingside and Queenside. When castling Kingside, the player moves their King two squares from the e-file to the g-file, and their King's Rook two squares from the h-file to the f-file; the move is written as O-O in chess notation.

The benefits of castling – on either side of the board – are several. The King escapes the centre of the board – where he may be vulnerable to attack because several of the Pawns around him will typically have advanced during the opening – and is placed in a corner, typically behind a wall of Pawns. The Rook, by contrast, in moving towards the centre, will be able to take full advantage of the open files the King has vacated.

Kingside castling is far more common than Queenside castling in top-level games, particularly with the White pieces; it is usually considered the safer option.

Positions before (above) and after (below) castling Kingside.

Castling Queenside
(O-O-O)

In Queenside castling, the White King moves from e1 to c1, and the White Queen's Rook moves from a1 to d1. (For Black, the King moves from e8 to c8 and the Rook from a8 to d8.) The move is written as O-O-O in chess notation.

Queenside castling is much less common than Kingside castling, particularly with the Black pieces. There may be several reasons for this. Queenside castling takes more time than Kingside castling, since three pieces need to be moved out of the way: not only the Knight and Bishop – as with Kingside castling – but also the Queen.

Additionally, since Queenside castling often leaves the a-Pawn unguarded, a further move may need to be spent moving the King to b1 (or b8) to defend it. Taking so much time to move your King to safety can be risky for either side, but particularly so for Black, who is always a move behind White. However, Queenside castling moves the Rook directly onto the important d-file, where it can be immediately effective, so this option has advantages as well as risks.

Castling on the same side as your opponent is typically the safer, more defensive option, since opposing Pawns cannot launch an advance on your King without exposing their own King. Castling on the opposite side to your opponent is therefore the more adventurous choice, enabling both sides to advance Pawns towards the opposition King.

Positions before (above) and after (below) Queenside castling.

En passant

Though Pawns can normally only make captures on squares diagonally in front of them – so the Black a-Pawn in the position pictured can only capture a piece on square b3 – there is an exception to this rule. This exception only comes into play when a Pawn advances two squares on its opening move, and thereby jumps over a square where it could be captured by an enemy Pawn (for instance if, in the position pictured, White moved their Pawn to b4).

In such positions, the opposing Pawn can respond as if the advancing Pawn had only moved a single square and can capture it 'en passant'. (The expression means 'in passing' in French.) It can do this only on the move immediately after the Pawn's advance. In making their move, the player removes the opposing Pawn from the board and places their own Pawn in the position the opposing Pawn would have occupied had it only advanced a single square. Thus, in the position pictured, White cannot safely advance the Pawn to b4, blocking Black's b-Pawn on b5 and placing the Black King in check, because Black simply responds by capturing the b-Pawn 'en passant' with their a-Pawn, almost certainly winning the game.

The 'en passant' rule is believed to have been one of the last major changes made to the rules of chess, added to compensate for an earlier change that allowed Pawns to advance two squares on their first move instead of just one.

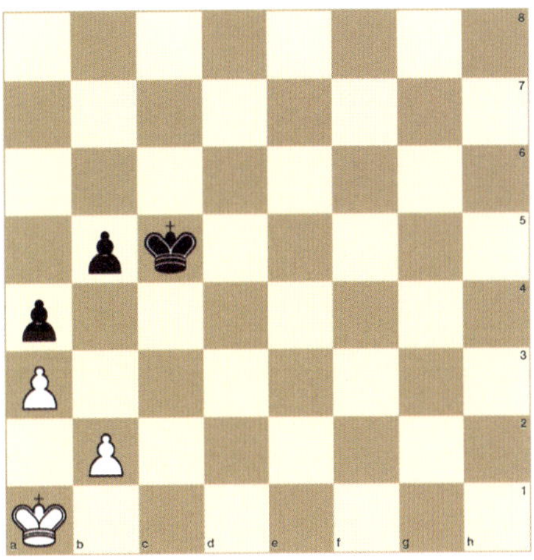

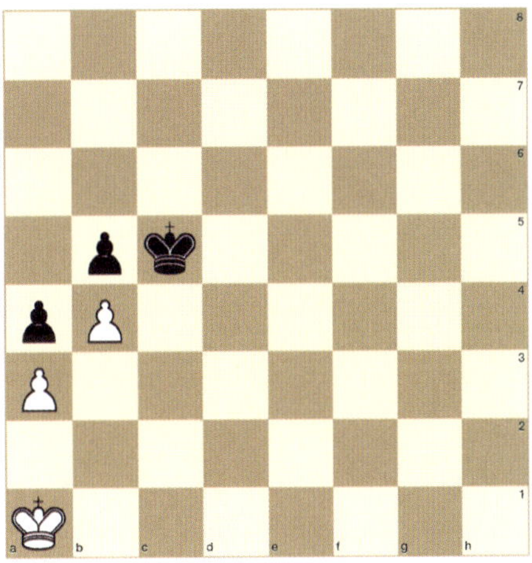

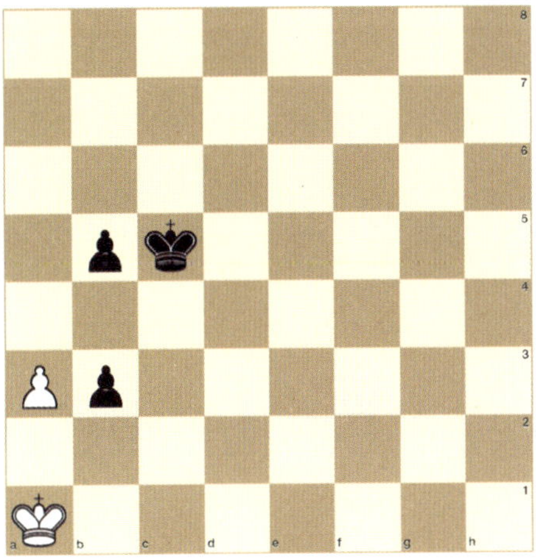

The first diagram (above left) shows the position before White's move. The second (above right) shows White moving their b-Pawn forward two squares, enabling Black to capture it 'en passant' in diagram three (below left).

Magnus Carlsen won five world chess championship titles before retiring undefeated in 2022.

FAMOUS PLAYERS

AND 10 CLASSIC GAMES

Asked to name the 10 greatest players of all time, 100 different people might produce 100 different lists. Indeed, they might produce more than 100: when Bobby Fischer chose his own top 10, once in 1964 and again in 1970, only six of the 10 names – Morphy, Staunton, Alekhine, Capablanca, Tal, and Reshevsky – featured on both lists. Certain names would surely recur in most people's selections – surely few would omit Fischer himself or Garry Kasparov – but many of the other places might seem open to debate. Some might draw on the official ratings to assert the contemporary claims of Fabiano Caruana, Levon Aronian, and Wesley So; others might argue the case for the great 19th-century figures of Wilhelm Steinitz, Howard Staunton, and Paul Morphy, whose brilliance pre-dates such calculations.

For that reason, then, this chapter does not pretend to offer a definitive list of the 10 greatest players; rather, it tells the stories of 10 of the most remarkable players ever to have lived, alongside an exciting game from each. They number nine world champions, and a prodigy who – though they never won that specific title – nevertheless spent more than 20 years as an undisputed world number one. Read on to find out who they are …

Emanuel Lasker was world chess champion for a record 27 years.

Emanuel Lasker

(1868–1941)

World champion for more than two decades – longer than any other player – Emanuel Lasker is widely regarded as one of the greatest players ever to have lived. He was born on Christmas Eve 1868 to Jewish parents in a small Prussian town in what is now part of Poland. At the age of 11 he moved to Berlin to study maths; he was something of a prodigy and would be awarded a doctorate in the subject in the early 1900s. There, he lived with his elder brother Berthold, who was studying medicine and taught him chess. The young Emanuel soon became a keen player.

Victory in a local Berlin tournament in 1889 with a stunning 20 wins out of 20 saw Lasker invited to the Schachbund Congress in Breslau, where he won the second-tier tournament – the 'Hauptturnier A' – thanks to a remarkable slice of luck. With two games to go, a player called Emil von Feyerfeil had a significant lead over Lasker, having already beaten him convincingly in an earlier round. However, an error in setting up the board when von Feyerfeil's penultimate game was resumed after an adjournment meant one of his pawns went missing; he lost the game, allowing Lasker to catch him in the final round and tie for first place. The resulting play-off saw Lasker win convincingly, assuming the title of 'Master' and becoming eligible to play in higher-level tournaments.

This was a turning point in his career. Travelling internationally, Lasker won tournaments in London and New York in 1892 and 1893 and also defeated several strong players

in matches. An ambitious request to challenge the 57-year-old reigning world champion Wilhelm Steinitz in 1894 was accepted, though Lasker struggled to raise the money required as a stake, and the match took place from March to May in New York, Philadelphia, and Montreal. After six games, the players were level at 3–3 before Lasker remarkably won five consecutive games; the challenger was crowned world champion on 26 May, having won 10 games to defeat Steinitz 12–7. A rematch two years later saw an even more convincing win for the younger man, by 12½ points to 4½ (and by 10 wins to two).

Following this victory, Lasker continued winning tournaments, but did not defend his world title for more than a decade, devoting his time instead to studying mathematics, receiving a doctorate in the subject in 1902. In 1907, however, he returned to match play in resounding fashion by thrashing the lively American challenger Frank J. Marshall by 11½ to 3½, not losing a single game. A year later, Lasker successfully defended his title again, this time against Siegbert Tarrasch, a player who had dismissively turned him down for a match back in 1892, insisting he should prove himself by winning a few international tournaments first. Lasker won four of the first five games and ultimately triumphed 10½–5½ (and by eight wins to three). Two more title defences followed in 1909 and 1910, with a convincing win for Laskar over Dawid Janowski (9½–1½) preceded by a much more challenging defence against the Austro-Hungarian player Carl Schlechter. With only one of the 10 scheduled games remaining, Lasker was a point behind his challenger, having drawn eight games and lost the other following a blunder. Only a victory in the final game would be enough for the reigning champion to tie the match and thus retain his title; a scrappy game ensued in which Schlechter missed chances both to win and to draw before ultimately losing.

After defeating the future world champions Capablanca and Alekhine in one of the most famous tournaments of all time in St. Petersburg in early 1914, Lasker played little chess during the First World War, which caused the cancellation of a proposed title defence against the Polish player Akiba Rubinstein and lost him the savings he had unwisely invested in German war bonds. Two years after the end of the war, however, the champion would give up his title in complicated circumstances. Having agreed to play Capablanca in a world title match in 1920, Lasker then abruptly resigned his title and awarded it to his would-be opponent; the following year, however, a title match nevertheless took place in Havana, Cuba, in which Lasker modestly insisted – to no great effect – that he was now the challenger and not the champion.

The match was a disappointment, though: four wins down after only 14 of the 30 scheduled games, Lasker resigned the series on grounds of ill health and returned to Europe, where he mostly abandoned chess in favour of maths and philosophy. He would also represent Germany at bridge, and wrote a play, *Vom Menschen die Geschichte* (*The History of Mankind*), with his brother. Forced to leave Germany in 1933 to escape Hitler's persecution of the Jews, Lasker moved first to England, then Moscow, and finally New York. These later years saw something of a renaissance in his chess career – which he resumed out of financial necessity – with strong performances in tournaments in Zurich, Moscow, and Nottingham. Lasker died in New York in January 1941, at the age of 72, and was buried in the Beth Olam Cemetery in Queens.

Lasker's approach to chess has been described as 'psychological', in the sense that he appeared to tailor his

moves not just to the position on the board, but also to the nature of his opponent. His critics used to claim that this led him sometimes to play deliberately poor moves purely to discombobulate his adversaries. The Austro-Hungarian player Richard Réti even wrote in an analysis of Lasker's play that he fought against his rivals not only intellectually but 'with the whole of his personality', a charge the champion vigorously denied. In the past few decades, however, several notable players, including Vladimir Kramnik, have dismissed such suggestions, arguing that this longest serving of all world champions was, in fact, ahead of his time: that only recently have the true strengths of his moves become as apparent to other players as they were to Laskar himself at the time.

LASKER 1 CAPABLANCA 0

ST. PETERSBURG, 1914

One of Lasker's most memorable games took place at one of the most famous tournaments of all time, St. Petersburg 1914. An unusual format saw 11 of the world's strongest players meet each other once in a preliminary competition, after which the top five progressed to a final round in which they played each other twice more. Points from the first competition were combined with those from the second, so when Capablanca won the opening round by 1½ points, the only player not to lose a game, he took that strong advantage with him into the second.

However, by the time Lasker met Capablanca for the final time – the pair having drawn their two previous games – he had almost caught up with his Cuban rival; the pair were level on points, but Lasker had only three games remaining to Capablanca's four. A win was therefore vital, and everyone expected the world champion to seek a complicated middle game in which tactics would come to the fore, while his opponent would try to simplify the game to claim the draw he needed. Instead, as White, Lasker allowed his opponent to exchange Queens as early as move six, and then embarked upon a slow positional game that offered Capablanca opportunities to play for an advantage. Placing his Knight deep into enemy territory on e6, Lasker enticed his opponent into making several slight but significant strategic errors until Black resigned on move 42 in a lost position.

Now leading by a point, but with one game fewer left to play, Lasker still needed his rival to slip up again to be sure of winning the tournament. Still shocked by his defeat, Capablanca lost his game in hand against Tarrasch and, despite winning his two final games, finished half a point behind the world champion.

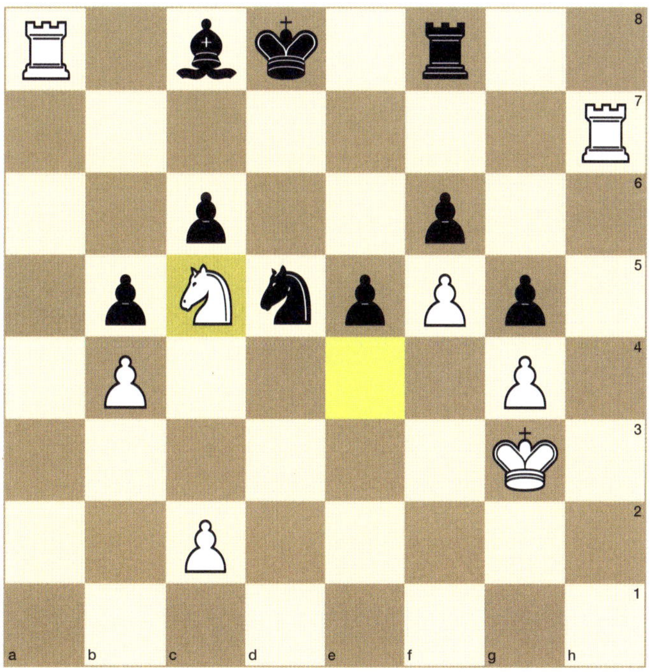

After 42 Nc5, Capablanca resigned, threatened with mate or the loss of a piece.

Between 10 February 1916 and 21 March 1924,
Capablanca did not lose a single game.

JOSÉ RAÚL CAPABLANCA

(1888–1942)

The man who assumed the title of world chess champion from Lasker, the Cuban José Raúl Capablanca, was born in the Castillo del Príncipe military fort in Havana on 19 November 1888. The young José taught himself to play by watching his father, a Spanish cavalry officer, playing against friends. In his memoir, Capablanca tells the story of how, at the age of four, he corrected his father after he made an illegal move; in disbelief at the discovery that the boy knew how to play, his father challenged him to a game and was defeated. Though medical advice prevented the young Capablanca from playing frequently, he nevertheless defeated the Cuban champion Juan Corzo in an eight-game match shortly after his 13th birthday.

After moving to New York in 1905 to study at Columbia, Capablanca abandoned his studies to focus entirely on chess. An eight-week tour of the United States in 1909 playing simultaneous matches against more than 600 opponents in 27 cities saw him lose just 13 games, and won him sponsorship for a match against Frank Marshall, who just two years earlier had challenged Lasker for the world title. Capablanca beat Marshall almost as convincingly as Lasker had, winning eight games to the older man's one. After this defeat, Marshall graciously insisted that his conqueror was invited to the prestigious San Sebastian tournament in Spain in 1911, despite Capablanca not having met the very strict entrance requirements; the young man won the tournament by half a point, ahead of most of the world's strongest players. Having proved his strength, Capablanca now challenged Lasker, who

had missed the tournament at San Sebastian, for the world chess championship. Though Lasker accepted the challenge, he presented the Cuban with so many conditions – including shorter sessions of play, a limit of 30 games, and the requirement for the challenger to win by a margin of two victories – that no agreement could be reached. Frustrated, Capablanca drafted a set of rules to govern future contests, which were agreed by the world's best players at the St. Petersburg tournament in 1914, where the two men met over the board for the very first time. Capablanca won the preliminary competition and was leading in the final when a defeat to Lasker threw him off his stride and cost him the tournament, which Lasker won instead.

The First World War put paid to any prospect of a title match for several years, but in 1920 the two great rivals agreed to play for the world championship the following year. Though – as we saw in the previous section – Lasker resigned his title to Capablanca before the match took place; and though, having reluctantly agreed to play the contest anyway, Lasker then withdrew halfway through the scheduled 30 games, the end result was still the same: José Raúl Capablanca was finally world chess champion, a mere decade after he had first challenged Lasker to a match.

The new rules Capablanca had drafted for the world championship required him to defend his title within a year against any challenger who could raise the sum of $10,000, but it would be six years before any match took place. Rubinstein, Nimzowitsch, and the Soviet émigré Alexander Alekhine all failed to raise the necessary funds, until a group of Argentinian businessmen – including the country's president – provided the backing required for a match between Alekhine and Capablanca. The contest began that September. Capablanca was the strong favourite: he had never lost to Alekhine, had been unbeaten for more than eight years until a defeat to Réti in 1924, and won that year's New York tournament by 2½ points from his challenger. Nevertheless, after 34 games over more than two months, the former Soviet – now a French citizen – defeated the Cuban by six wins to three. Capablanca's reign was over.

Having lost his title, Capablanca returned to tournament play, winning several competitions in the absence of his conqueror, whom he would not face over the board for almost a decade (by which point Alekhine had lost his title to the Dutchman Max Euwe). High blood pressure hampered his attempt to win the right to challenge Euwe for the title at the AVRO tournament in 1938, and his outstanding performance in the 1939 Olympiad in Buenos Aires – in which he was awarded the gold medal for the highest score on the top board – was his last. On 7 March 1942, aged only 53, Capablanca suffered a cerebral haemorrhage watching a casual game of chess at the New York Chess Club, and died the following morning at the same Mount Sinai hospital where his predecessor as world champion, Emanuel Lasker, had died the year before.

Capablanca's style of play has been dismissed as 'riskless' and lacking in adventure, resulting at times in such a high proportion of draws that sneering disapproval from his fellow players – Euwe once observed that his rival was 'not sparing in attempts to agree to a draw' – was joined by frustration from spectators; a 13-move draw with Rubinstein in a 1922 tournament in London was especially notorious. Alekhine was particularly scathing of the man he replaced as champion: in his book on the 1927 New York tournament that preceded his capture of Capablanca's title, in what the British player William Hartston describes as 'one of the greatest character assassinations in chess literature', he dismissed his beaten opponent as 'great only in defence' and 'not to be feared by a first-rate master'.

Yet to many other players and commentators Capablanca remains one of the greatest players of all time. The author and *New York Times* chess correspondent Harold C. Schonberg, whose chapter on Capablanca in his book *Grandmasters of Chess* is titled 'The Chess Machine', describes him as 'the Mozart of chess – pure, classic, elegant, subtle, refined ... the master of masters, the complete technician'. Perhaps the final word should go to Emanuel Lasker, the man he replaced as world champion; talking to a friend shortly after losing his title, Lasker said that of all the players he had known, Capablanca was the 'one chess genius'.

CAPABLANCA 1 SPIELMANN 0
NEW YORK, 1927

The 1927 New York tournament pitted world champion Capablanca against five of the strongest players of the time, including Alexander Alekhine, who would deprive him of his title later that year. Each player played the others four times, twice with White and twice with Black, resulting in a marathon 20-round competition that lasted for more than a month. Capablanca won the tournament convincingly, remaining undefeated and finishing a clear 2½ points ahead of second-placed Alekhine, a result that may have made him complacent in the title match that followed.

It is his win against the Austrian Rudolf Spielmann, known variously as the 'Last Romantic' or the 'Master of Attack', that has lived longest in the memory, however – its striking Bishop sacrifice winning Capablanca the 'brilliancy' prize for the tournament's best game.

Playing White, Capablanca opened with 1 d4 and the resulting Queen's Gambit Declined saw Black give up the Bishop pair in exchange for an advanced and seemingly strong string of Pawns on the Queen's side. However, on move 18 Capablanca sacrificed a Bishop, refusing to defend it and capturing Black's b-Pawn instead. Then, when Black duly captured the Bishop with his Queen, White responded by taking a second Pawn with his remaining Bishop, winning a third when Black was forced to move his newly threatened Rook. Suddenly Capablanca had not only three Pawns for his Bishop but also an a-Pawn on the sixth rank, only two squares away from becoming a Queen. Black's frantic retaliatory attack on White's King's side, advancing the Bishop to h3 in the hope of mating on g2, was never likely to succeed, and Spielmann resigned on move 26, with his Queen and Knight both under attack and White's a-Pawn on the verge of becoming a Queen.

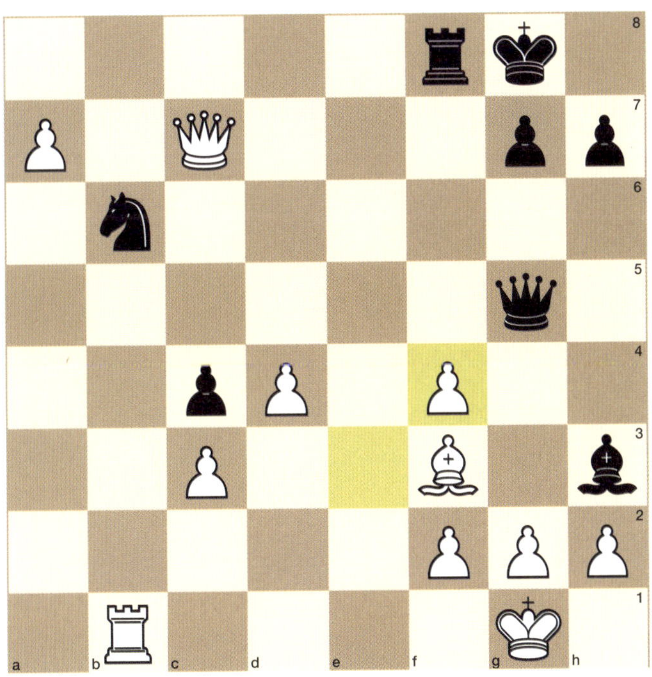

Spielmann resigned after 26 exf4, because he could not prevent White's a-Pawn from becoming a Queen without losing his own Queen.

In 1937, Alexander Alekhine became the first player to regain the world chess championship by defeating Max Euwe.

ALEXANDER ALEKHINE

(1892–1946)

Capablanca's conqueror had been born into privilege in Moscow, his father a Russian landowner and politician, his mother an heiress. By the age of 16, Alexander Alekhine had won the 1909 All-Russian Amateur Championship held in St. Petersburg, and steady improvement over the next five years saw him win tournaments of gradually increasing strength – mostly in that same city, where he had lived since 1911 – before finishing third behind Lasker and Capablanca at the famous St. Petersburg tournament of 1914.

Alekhine's life was rarely straightforward. He suffered a double misfortune when playing a tournament in Mannheim, Germany, at the start of the First World War; not only was the competition abandoned – he had been leading at the time, on course for his first international victory – but he then also spent a month interned as a prisoner of war in the German town of Rastatt before being allowed to return home to Russia. Following the revolution, he travelled to Ukraine, where he spent time in a death cell in Odesa on suspicion of espionage, before being once again released. Marrying his second wife in 1921 barely a year after he had married (and then divorced) his first – and, as a result, gaining permission to travel outside communist Russia – Alekhine left the country with her almost immediately, then deserted her in Paris four months later, moving to Berlin.

For the next six years, Alekhine played tournaments and matches all over the world, winning most of them, all the while trying to raise the $10,000 purse that the Cuban world champion Capablanca required to grant him a shot at the title. The match finally took place in 1927 in Buenos Aires, when a group of Argentinian businessmen raised the necessary funds. The winner would be the first to six victories, and though Alekhine won the

opening game, Capablanca won two and drew four of the next six games to lead 2–1 after seven. It would, however, be another 22 games until he won another: three draws were followed by two successive victories for Alekhine; eight more draws were followed by another Alekhine win, and then came another seven successive draws before the last of Capablanca's victories. That left Alekhine with only the narrowest of leads – 4–3 – but two wins as White in the next five games saw the former Russian take the title by six wins to three. At 34 games – of which an unprecedented 25 were draws – this was by far the longest championship match so far, and it would remain so for more than five decades, until – as we shall later read – Anatoly Karpov's 1984–85 defence of his title against Garry Kasparov was controversially abandoned after 48 games.

After his victory, Alekhine immediately offered the Cuban a rematch, but – pointedly – only on the terms he had himself been forced to accept. When Capablanca proved unable to raise the funds required, Alekhine agreed to play another former Russian: Efim Bogoljubow, who had played alongside him at that Mannheim tournament, had been interned for rather longer, and was now a German citizen. Bogoljubow was not, however, the strongest of challengers, and was convincingly beaten – under a new system that required the victor to win six games and score more than 15 points – by 11 victories to five, and 15½–9½ on points. A second match, under the same system, took place in 1934, and was barely any closer: Alekhine won 15½–10½ and by eight wins to three.

Alekhine's third defence of his title, the following year, would prove more problematic. His challenger this time was the Dutchman Max Euwe – a strong player, but not one widely expected to trouble the champion – and after seven games, the holder led by four victories to one. Over the next seven games, however, Euwe levelled the scores, and though Alekhine soon took another two-point lead, wins for Euwe in games 20 and 21 brought the scores level once more. Two more wins for the challenger in games 25 and 26 left him on the brink of the title, and even a victory for Alekhine in the following game was not enough to prevent Euwe taking the title after 30 games by nine wins to eight, and 15½–14½ on points.

Alekhine had been drinking heavily during the contest – as he himself admitted – and when Euwe graciously accepted a return match, the former champion sobered up and got to work preparing. After five games of the rematch – which took place across 12 Dutch cities in 1937 – Euwe led by two victories to one, but Alekhine won four of the next five games, and then four of the last five, too, to reclaim his title by a convincing 10 wins to four, and 15½–9½ on points. This would be his final title match, however: negotiations for matches with Capablanca and the Russian challenger Mikhail Botvinnik were put on hold after the outbreak of the Second World War, and though a contest with the latter was later confirmed for 1946, Alekhine died of a heart attack in a Portugal hotel room before it could take place. He was 53.

After defeating Euwe, Alekhine played no further championship matches and thus held the title until his death in 1946.

A controversial figure with a complex personal morality – he was accused of collaboration with the Nazis during the war – Alekhine was nevertheless a remarkable player. His fierce attacking style made powerful use of ingenious tactical

combinations: forced sequences of moves, often containing a sacrifice, which resulted in a significant advantage. Those moments of tactical genius, however, required a deep positional awareness that could identify long-distant future possibilities that remained invisible to other, lesser players. His influence on the game has been enduring. Not only did he give his name to the opening Alekhine's Defence (1 e4 Nf6), along with variations in a wide range of other openings including the Ruy Lopez Exchange Variation and the Dutch Defence, but he also inspired future generations of champions. Garry Kasparov – world champion from 1985 to 2000 – once predicted that 'the future belongs to "Alekhine chess"'.

RÉTI 0 ALEKHINE 1
BADEN-BADEN, 1925

Having started out as a somewhat conventional, if highly tactical, player Richard Réti transformed himself after the First World War into one of the principal proponents of the 'hypermodern' school of chess, which encouraged players to leave the centre of the board vacant of Pawns so that it could be controlled from afar by distant pieces. His decision to play 1 g7 – the King's Fianchetto opening – in his game as White against Alekhine at the 1925 Baden-Baden tournament was therefore entirely characteristic. The year before this tournament, Réti had achieved one of his greatest successes, beating both Alekhine and Capablanca at the famous New York Tournament of 1924, so his opponent would have known he was in for a challenging game. It was a game that would be won by an attack of absolute brilliance.

A complex middle game saw White develop significant attacking opportunities on the Queen's side, where most of his pieces were gathered, while Black had some compensatory threats on the King's side. Suddenly, however, Black advanced his Rook to e3, where it could seemingly be captured by White's f-Pawn. The point of this apparent sacrifice was two-fold. It could not be accepted, since if White captured the Rook with the f-Pawn, Black would immediately capture with his Queen the g-Pawn that it had been defending, threatening a mate that White could at best only delay at the cost of his Queen. But if the Rook remained where it was, it would simply capture the g-Pawn anyway and prompt the same conclusion. Réti was forced to block the threat with his Knight, upon which Alekhine continued his attack with relentless audacity, leaving his Rook under threat for a further five moves as he built up a series of threats that would eventually see his hypermodernist opponent resign on move 42 facing the unavoidable loss of a Knight.

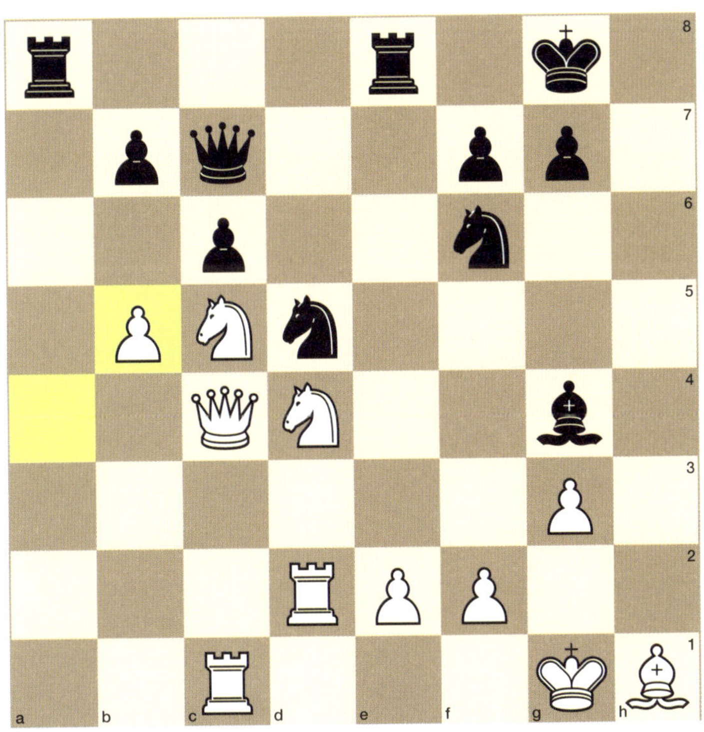

After 26 axb4, Alekhine played 26 … Re3. Black's Rook cannot be captured (27 fxe3) because White will capture the Pawn on g3 with his Queen, threatening mate.

Mikhail Botvinnik won the world title five times, but also lost two championship matches.

MIKHAIL BOTVINNIK (1911–95)

The man who would ultimately succeed Alekhine as world chess champion – and who would be the first of the Soviet-era champions – was born in 1911 in Kuokkala, just outside St. Petersburg. His Russian Jewish parents worked as dentists, and Botvinnik, who became a 'convinced communist' at the age of nine, would later describe his identity as 'complicated', considering himself 'a Jew by blood, a Russian by culture, Soviet by upbringing'. Taught chess by a friend of his brother, he soon caught the eye of Nikolai Krylenko, head of the Soviet chess association, who had been tasked with improving the nation's chess as a demonstration of its intellectual superiority over the decadent West. When the then world champion Capablanca came to Moscow in 1925 to take part in a tournament organized by Krylenko, he visited Leningrad (as St. Petersburg had been renamed the previous year) to play a simultaneous exhibition. The young Botvinnik won his game against the champion, who predicted that he would enjoy an excellent future.

In 1927, aged 16, he became the youngest player to take part in the USSR Chess Championship, sharing fifth place; four years later, he won the first of his six Soviet titles. Now identified as the nation's greatest prospect for the world championship, he started to play internationally, drawing a match against the Czech champion Salo Flohr and finishing ahead of both Lasker and Capablanca in the 1935 Moscow tournament, which he won jointly with Flohr. The following year, in Nottingham, Botvinnik became the first Soviet player to win a tournament outside his own country, sharing victory with Capablanca and finishing ahead of both Euwe – the current

world champion – and Alekhine. When Alekhine regained his title in 1937, negotiations soon began for Botvinnik to challenge him, but the outbreak of the Second World War put the match on hold.

Alekhine's death in 1946 created considerable problems in determining his successor, since the championship had always previously been decided by a match between the holder and a challenger. For two years there was no world champion at all, until it was eventually decided that a tournament between the strongest contenders would decide the title. Botvinnik thus joined Dutch former champion Max Euwe, the American Samuel Reshevsky, and his fellow Soviets Vasily Smyslov and Paul Keres in a marathon 25-round tournament held jointly in The Hague and Moscow from March to May 1948. At the end, the man from Kuokkala was crowned as the sixth world chess champion, having led from the start and finishing three full points ahead of his compatriot Smyslov in second, achieving eight wins and suffering only two defeats.

Botvinnik became world champion by winning the 1948 tournament set up to find a successor to Alekhine.

Having won his title unconventionally via a tournament, Botvinnik would defend it more conventionally, playing seven matches over the next 15 years, though his grip was rarely firm. In his first defence in 1951, against his fellow Soviet David Bronstein, defeats in games 21 and 22 left him on the brink of losing the title before a win and a draw in the final two games saw him scrape the 12–12 draw that allowed him to retain his crown. Three years later, his second defence, against Smyslov, was only slightly more comfortable: leading by two points with five games to go, Botvinnik lost twice in four games, leaving him needing a draw in the final game to achieve another 12–12 tie. After two matches in which he had held onto his title by the narrowest of margins, the champion's luck ran out in 1957 when he once again faced Smyslov; this time, the challenger won convincingly 12½–9½, and by six wins to three; Botvinnik's reign as world chess champion was over.

Or rather, it was interrupted. The rules at the time still allowed a defeated champion a rematch, and a third consecutive title match between Botvinnik and Smyslov took place the following year: starting strongly with three wins in a row, the dethroned champion held a four-point lead with six games to go, and though defeats in games 19 and 22 threatened to throw him off course, he ultimately held his nerve to defeat his former conqueror 12½–10½, and by seven wins to five. Having regained his title with his first clear match victory – at the fourth attempt – Botvinnik would face a new challenger in 1960: Mikhail Tal, another Soviet. This time, however, Botvinnik was beaten convincingly, three wins behind after only seven games, and ultimately winning only two of 22 games in a 12½–8½ defeat. Once again, though, the champion was entitled to a rematch, and once again Botvinnik took full advantage of this rule. A second match with Tal took place in 1961, and this time the result was reversed: Botvinnik won 13–8, and by 10 wins to five, to regain his title and become to date the oldest man to win a championship match, at 49.

This rule had been changed by the time of Botvinnik's final title defence, against Tigran Petrosian in 1963, and so a 12½–9½ defeat (by five wins to two) marked the end of his reign. He withdrew from the contest to produce a challenger to the new champion and retired from chess entirely in 1970, devoting himself to working with the next generation of Soviet players – including both Karpov and Kasparov – and developing computer chess programmes. He died in 1995, aged 83.

The first Soviet world champion, Botvinnik marked the beginning of an era of Soviet dominance of the championship that would last – with one brief but explosive exception – from 1948 to the collapse of the Soviet Union in 1991. His strategic approach to the game made him a phenomenally dangerous opponent – Raymond Keene and Nathan Divinsky rated him the fourth strongest player of all time – yet he was never the most commanding of champions: despite winning the vacant title with a commanding tournament victory, and holding on to it for 13 of the next 15 years, he never won a defence outright, drawing two matches and losing three; his only title victories came as challenger, when he had lost his crown.

BOTVINNIK 1 CAPABLANCA 0
ROTTERDAM, 1938

The AVRO tournament of 1938 was intended to establish an unofficial challenger for Alexander Alekhine as world champion. Taking place over 22 days across 10 Dutch cities, it featured the eight strongest players in the world – including Alekhine himself – with each playing twice against the others. Having drawn their first game, Botvinnik and Capablanca met again in the 11th round, with both players at least a point behind the leaders. The game – which featured two remarkable sacrifices by the future world champion – would become known as one of the greatest of all time.

Playing White, Botvinnik opened with 1 d4, and the game became a Nimzo-Indian Defence, with both players castling on the King's side and advancing on the Queen's side. After 30 moves, White was a Pawn down but with a passed King's Pawn on e6 by way of compensation. Suddenly, however, Botvinnik moved his Bishop from b2 – where it had spent almost the entire game stuck behind a chain of Pawns along the long diagonal – to a3, where it threatened Black's Queen, but could be captured itself. Black duly captured the Bishop with his Queen – the alternative options were no better – which left him short of pieces to defend on the King's side, as Botvinnik had intended. He responded with a second sacrifice, giving check with his Knight from a square where it could be captured by Black's Pawn. When the Knight too was taken, White moved his Queen to check the King itself and so win back the Knight, before advancing the e-Pawn to within a square of becoming a Queen. Black's only defence against the inevitable was to chase White's King around the board with a series of checks, but Botvinnik had seen ahead so clearly that he knew that these checks would eventually run out. The moment they did, Capablanca resigned.

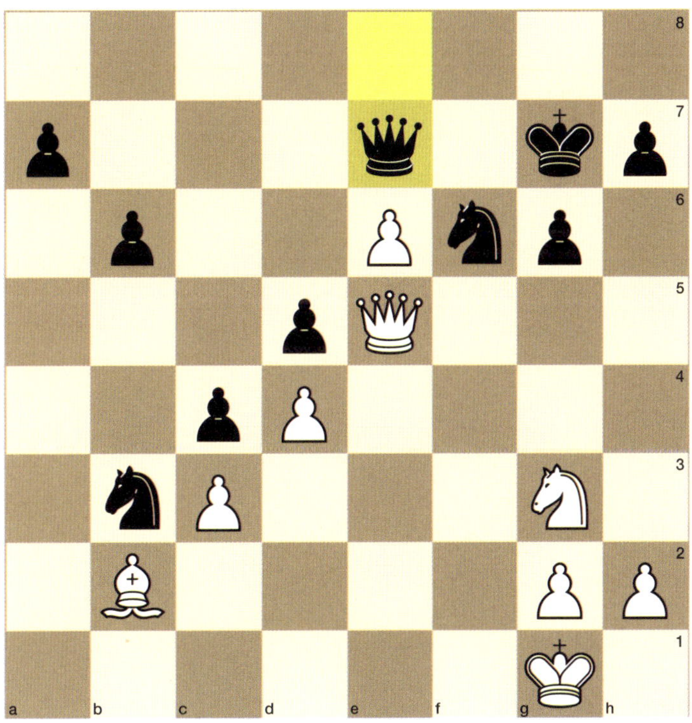

After Capablanca's 29 … Qe7, Botvinnik played 30 Ba3, forcing Black to capture the Bishop, and then 31 Nh5+, sacrificing two pieces for a winning attack.

The eighth world chess champion, Mikhail Tal held the title for only 371 days.

MIKHAIL TAL
(1936–92)

Though Mikhail Tal held the world championship for just a single year, losing his title to Botvinnik in May 1961 even more decisively than he had won it from him 12 months earlier, he remains one of the most thrillingly attacking and inventive players of all time. His aggressive style, full of complex combinations and unexpected sacrifices, was risky and often flawed – as post-game analysis would sometimes demonstrate – but was usually brutally effective in practice, making him the youngest ever world champion at the age of only 23.

Born into a Jewish family in Latvia in 1936, Tal was a prodigious talent. Aged 14, he qualified for the Latvian championship; by the time he was 16, he was his nation's champion. As a 19-year-old in 1956, he finished joint fifth in the Soviet National Championship – Latvia had been occupied by the Soviet Union since 1944 – and the following year he added this title to his collection, defeating along the way both Paul Keres – who had been one of five candidates for the vacant world title in 1948 – and the beaten 1951 world championship challenger David Bronstein. Retaining his title the following year, Tal also entered the world championship qualifying cycle that had since 1950 decided which player won the right to challenge the champion, replacing the previous system of would-be contenders having to find $10,000 to take on the titleholder. Winning the 1958 Interzonal Tournament in Switzerland qualified him for the next stage of the contest, the 1959 Candidates' Tournament in Yugoslavia. Tal won this too, finishing a clear 1½ points ahead of runner-up Paul Keres; defeating his fellow qualifier, the 16-year-old future champion Bobby Fischer, in all four of their games; and so intimidating his opponent Pal Benko with his fierce stare that the former Hungarian Grandmaster wore dark glasses

Tal was a brilliant attacking player whose risky style made him a formidable opponent.

to a later game between the pair. In response, Tal borrowed a comically large pair of sunglasses from a spectator, prompting laughs from the crowd, and still won the game.

And so, in 1960, aged only 23, Tal found himself playing Mikhail Botvinnik, more than twice his age, for the world championship title. The pair had never met before, and few observers thought the young Latvian stood much chance against the four-time champion. The match took place in Moscow, and Tal started strongly, winning the opening game and then two more in short order, one after the brilliant sacrifice of a knight. Three points ahead after seven games, he then lost two games in a row, but three wins and no defeats in the remainder of the match saw him crowned world champion with three games to spare, by six wins to two, and 12½–8½.

The inevitable rematch was also played in Moscow, but this time Tal was facing two opponents: not only Botvinnik – who had spent the intervening year examining his rival's style in minute detail, and who consequently took every opportunity to move the play away from the fast-moving tactical positions Tal enjoyed, towards the slow positional struggles he personally preferred – but also his own health. Weeks before the match was due to start, Tal had spent some time in hospital suffering from kidney problems; some sources suggest he had also suffered a mild heart attack. His own doctors had advised him to seek a postponement on health grounds, but Botvinnik is said to have insisted that he be examined by doctors in Moscow before any delay could be agreed. Rather than submit to such indignities, Tal decided to play the match regardless, and paid the price, losing 10 times in 21 games to lose the match 13–8, and by 10 wins to five. After barely a year, his reign as world champion was over.

Though Tal would continue to play in the world championship qualifying cycle for the next three decades, he would never again challenge directly for the title, losing in the candidates' final in 1965, the semi-final in 1968, and the quarter-final in 1980. Soviet champion six times between 1957 and 1978, he would also play for the victorious Soviet team in eight Olympiads, losing only two out of 101 games, and adding five individual gold medals – for the best score on a particular board – and two silvers to his eight team golds. After the break-up of the Soviet Union, Tal would be denied the opportunity to represent his native Latvia in their first Olympiad in June 1992, however, due to ill health. Three days after the tournament concluded, and barely a month after defeating world champion Garry Kasparov in 17 moves in a blitz match, he died in Moscow at the age of 55. His health had continued to be problematic throughout his career, no doubt complicated by his enthusiastic smoking and drinking – William Hartston tells a story of him drinking brandies until four in the morning during a tournament in Holland then winning convincingly in a game that started four hours later – and he had had a kidney removed in 1969, which prompted a return to good form that saw him win tournaments in Sochi, Tallinn, Wijk aan Zee, and Baku over the next few years.

Nicknamed the 'Magician from Riga' on account of his flair for unexpected tactical brilliancies, Tal moderated his approach to the game in later life, developing a more positional style that served him well in the late 1970s and early 1980s. His obituary in the *New York Times* described him as 'one of the game's most popular and exciting players', lacking the ego of many of his contemporaries, while in 2005, world champion Kramnik labelled him a 'real chess genius' who played primarily for fun rather than out of ambition. His reign as world champion may have been brief, but his reputation has lasted.

TAL 1 SMYSLOV 0

BLED (SLOVENIA), 1959

The 1959 Candidates Tournament, held to find the latest challenger for four-time world champion Mikhail Botvinnik, took place over almost two months across three cities in what was then Yugoslavia. Each competitor played his seven rivals four times, with former champion Vasily Smyslov, veteran of three title matches already, one of the pre-tournament favourites. Mikhail Tal, his opponent in his first-round game, was not to be underestimated, having won the Interzonal tournament to reach this stage, but Smyslov weathered his opponent's initial attack to win quite comfortably.

By the time the players met again in the eighth round, Tal had recovered from this early setback to share the lead with Keres and Petrosian; Smyslov, by contrast, had not won again and was sharing fifth place. Playing White this time, Tal opened with 1 e4 and his opponent replied with the Caro-Kann. Exchanging both sets of central Pawns early on opened up the board for the major pieces. Castling on opposite sides then gave both players opportunities to launch attacks on the enemy Kings – just the sort of sharp, tactical battle at which Tal excelled. On move 14, he offered a Bishop sacrifice which Smyslov accepted only to be forced to return it a few moves later. On move 19, with Black's Queen stuck on the wrong side of the board attempting a lone attack on White's King, Tal took advantage of a lax move by his opponent to sacrifice his Queen. To stave off the threat of immediate mate, Smyslov had no choice but to return the Queen a few moves later and would emerge with a hopeless position, resigning on move 26. Encouraged by this victory, Tal went on to win the tournament by a point and a half, earning the right to challenge Botvinnik for the world title.

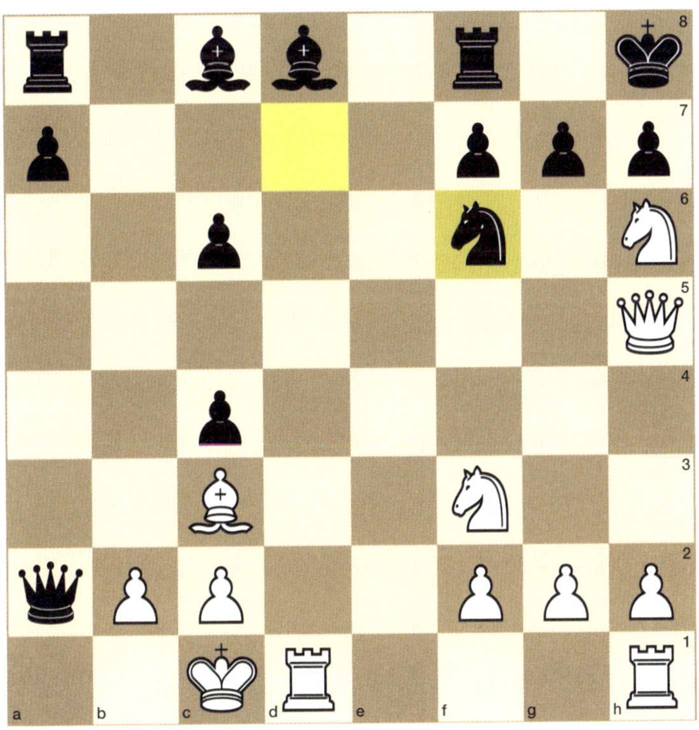

After Smyslov's 18 … Nf6, Tal (as White) played 19 Qxf7, offering to sacrifice his Queen for a winning attack. Black resigned a few moves later.

To many, Bobby Fischer is the greatest chess player of all time.

BOBBY FISCHER
(1943–2008)

When Bobby Fischer died in January 2008 at the age of 64, the words 'legend' and 'genius' recurred so often in his obituaries that they might have been dictated by the man himself. The chapter on Fischer in William Hartston's book *The Kings of Chess* is titled 'The Greatest of Them All', and for many players, fans, and writers, Fischer was precisely that. The obituaries, however, also highlighted another side of this phenomenal player, labelling him 'troubled', 'enigmatic', or 'controversial'. Bobby Fischer may have been the greatest player ever, but he also sought out conflict and controversy in ways that first enhanced his reputation, but which would ultimately tarnish it.

Born in Chicago in 1943 to parents who divorced two years later, Fischer was brought up by his mother, moving to Manhattan at the age of six. He was soon playing chess at local clubs, and in 1956 he not only won the United States Junior Championship, becoming the competition's youngest ever champion at the age of 13, but also tied for fourth place in his first U.S. Open Championship.

The following year, Fischer successfully defended his junior title and surpassed his achievement at the previous year's U.S. Open, winning the championship on a tie-break to become that tournament's youngest ever winner too. Invited to take part in the 1957–58 U.S. Championship, Fischer continued his outstanding run of form to win that competition as well, becoming, at the age of 14, the youngest ever U.S. champion. He would go on to win that tournament seven more times – every time he played in it – and in 1963–64 would achieve the

A young Bobby Fischer plays a game at New York's Manhattan Chess Club.

only perfect score in the competition's history, winning all 11 of his games.

Fischer's victory in the 1957–58 U.S. Championship was his ticket to the world championship qualification cycle; finishing sixth in his first Interzonal tournament, he qualified for the following year's Candidates Tournament where, still only 16, he finished joint fifth out of eight. Three years later in 1962, he would win the Interzonal convincingly, by a margin of 2½ points from Efim Geller, but only finished fourth in the Candidates Tournament, behind a trio of Soviets: Petrosian, Keres, and Geller. Outraged by what he considered to be collusion between this group, who drew all 12 of their games against each other, Fischer alleged not only that they cynically pre-arranged those draws to save their energies for other opponents, but also that a fifth Soviet, Victor Korchnoi, deliberately lost his games against the group to ensure that they finished ahead of their Western competitors; he even additionally suggested that players consulted with each other during their games. His allegations would have two consequences: firstly, the Candidates Tournament was replaced with a series of knock-out matches that would make such collusion impossible in future, and secondly – despite this change – the furious Fischer boycotted the next championship qualification cycle in protest.

Consequently, it was not until 1967 that Fischer would again compete – albeit briefly – for the chance to challenge the world champion, now Tigran Petrosian. This time, he was leading the Interzonal tournament after 10 rounds when a disagreement over rest days saw him first default two games and then withdraw entirely.

By the time the next Interzonal came around in 1970, Fischer was keen to take part, but his contrary nature had created an obstacle: having boycotted the 1969 U.S. Championship over an entirely unrelated dispute, he was not one of the designated American qualifiers. However, in an act of patriotic selflessness that Fischer, ironically, might not perhaps have approved of had it taken place in the Soviet Union, first Pal Benko and then William Lombardy withdrew from the cycle so that Fischer could compete as one of the American representatives.

After his world championship victory in 1972, Fischer would not play another competitive game for almost 20 years.

He won the Interzonal tournament decisively – 3½ points ahead of the second-placed Bent Larsen – and then thrashed the Soviet Mark Taimanov 6–0 in the Candidates quarter-final, repeating the feat against Larsen in the semi-final. The former world champion Tigran Petrosian put up more of a fight in the final but was beaten 6½–2½; Fischer had finally earned himself the right to challenge for the championship, against the Soviet Boris Spassky, who had won the title from Petrosian in 1969.

The resulting world championship match, held in Iceland in 1972, was not short on controversy. By now, players from the Soviet Union had held the title for 24 years, through Botvinnik, Smyslov, Tal, Petrosian, and Spassky: Fischer thus became the West's great hope in its struggle to seize the symbolic title from its Cold War rival.

The match was first postponed a few days when Fischer quibbled over cash; then, after losing the opening game from a drawn position, he forfeited the second in a dispute over playing conditions; when his requests for changes were granted, he returned to the board, now already two points behind, and proceeded to win three of the next four games to take the lead. Three more wins in the next seven games – and a solitary defeat – saw Fischer leading 8–5 after 13 games; seven consecutive draws then left him one win from the title, which he duly delivered in game 21. By seven wins to three, and 12½–8½, Fischer was at last world champion.

That final win would be Fischer's last competitive game for almost 20 years. When Anatoly Karpov emerged as his challenger in 1974, the organizers' refusal to accept the champion's demands – for a match in which only wins counted, with the winner being the first to 10 victories, and the holder retaining the title if the score reached 9–9 – prompted Fischer to

resign his title. His self-imposed exile from the board continued until 1992, when a controversial rematch with Spassky took place in Yugoslavia. Fischer won 10–5 but was issued with an arrest warrant for breaking U.S. sanctions on the war-torn country. Disappearing first to Japan and then to Iceland – having spent almost a year in a Japanese jail for using a revoked passport – he became increasingly obsessed with conspiracy theories. A genius he most certainly was, but – as his obituaries noted – a very troubled genius.

BYRNE 0 FISCHER 1
NEW YORK, 1956

The game between 13-year-old Bobby Fischer and the 26-year-old International Master and former U.S. Open champion Donald Byrne was christened 'The Game of the Century' almost as soon as it had been played. It took place at the Marshall Chess Club in New York, as part of the third Rosenwald Memorial Tournament, and was one of only two victories the young Fischer would enjoy in his 11 games.

Playing Black, Fischer encouraged his opponent to occupy the centre while he exerted pressure from the margins, tempting his opponent to overreach himself and advance too far. On move 11, he offered White a Knight sacrifice that Byrne wisely declined, instead retreating his Queen to the edge of the board. Two moves later, Fischer made his opponent another offer, tempting him with the chance to win a Rook for a Bishop; this too was declined, but a third and greater sacrifice was imminent. Happy to leave his pieces under threat in search of further, winning complications, Fischer then on move 17 ignored an attack on his Queen, sacrificing her to bring another piece into the attack and prompt a series of repeated checks from Knight and Bishop that allowed him to win so many pieces in return for the Queen – a Rook, two Bishops, and a Pawn – that White's position was entirely hopeless after only 25 moves. Though Byrne played on, perhaps in shock, until he was elegantly mated on move 41 – Black's Rook, Knight, and two Bishops all acting in concert – he had been lost for a long time already.

This win brought Fischer to public attention; he appeared on the cover of *Chess Review* with the caption 'The Game of the Century', and a page of the magazine was devoted to analysing the game. He was now famous; in little more than a year, he would win his first United States Championship.

In reply to Byrne's 17 Kf1, Fischer ignored the attack on his Queen to play the brilliant 17 … Be6, sacrificing his Queen in return for so much material that White's position was soon lost.

Anatoly Karpov played in seven world championship matches between 1978 and 1990.

ANATOLY KARPOV

(BORN 1951)

The player who stepped into Bobby Fischer's shoes to become the 12th world chess champion could scarcely have been more different from his predecessor. Where Bobby Fischer might sometimes have seemed the epitome of American individualism, Anatoly Karpov was very much the establishment Soviet man; where Fischer had dropped out of school at the age of 16 to devote himself to chess, Karpov studied maths and economics at universities in Leningrad and Moscow; and where Fischer won his title by beating the previous champion then refused to defend it, not playing a competitive game for almost 20 years, Karpov inherited the championship without a title match but then would play in seven further contests over the next 15 years (and three more after the world championship split in 1993).

Both players were prodigies, however. Born in 1951 in Western Russia, Karpov learned to play chess at four and by the age of 12 was an attendee at a prestigious chess school run by Mikhail Botvinnik, the former world champion. He became world junior champion in 1969, the first Soviet to do so since Spassky in 1955, and made his debut in the following year's Soviet Championship, finishing joint fifth.

His world junior championship earned him entry to the Leningrad Interzonal, the first stage of the world championship qualification cycle, where Karpov tied for first place to reach the Candidates Tournament. There, he played three of his compatriots, defeating Lev Polugaevsky in the quarter-final, newly dethroned former champion Boris Spassky in the semi-final, and Viktor Korchnoi in the final, by the narrowest of margins: leading by three wins to zero with six games to go,

Karpov lost twice in the next three matches and only three draws secured him the right to challenge Fischer.

When Fischer conceded his title, Karpov was appointed champion by default. He responded with a string of tournament victories, and by the time he faced the first defence of his title in 1978 – against Korchnoi, the player who had pushed him so hard in the Candidates final three years earlier – he was broadly accepted as a legitimate world champion. This time, six wins would be required for victory, and once again Karpov wobbled with victory in sight: leading convincingly by five wins to two after 27 games, he then lost three out of the next four before one final victory got him over the finishing line. His second title defence, also against Korchnoi, would prove much easier: this time, the champion needed only 18 games to reach six victories, losing only two games en route.

Karpov's first world title defence took place in 1978 in Baguio, the Philippines, against Viktor Korchnoi.

Initially, Karpov's third title defence, against his fellow Soviet, the young, iconoclastic Garry Kasparov, in 1984, seemed to be a similar mismatch: after nine games, the champion had already established a four-point lead, and needed just two more wins to retain his title. Would this be the shortest championship match of all time? However, a fifth win proved elusive, arriving only after a record 17 consecutive draws, and chances to win a decisive sixth were wasted in games 31 and 41. Kasparov had by this point notched a win of his own – leaving him 5–1 behind after a remarkable 35 draws – and would swiftly win two games in a row to leave Karpov once again wobbling. At this point, the authorities stepped in and halted the match, citing concerns for the champion's health. This longest championship match of all time – at 48 games – had begun in September, and it was now February: a rematch, limited to 24 games, would take place in September.

The second match began with a win for Kasparov, before consecutive wins for Karpov turned the tables; at the halfway point, the scores were level, but two more wins for Kasparov, and only one for Karpov, left the champion needing a win with White in the final game to tie the match 12–12 and retain his title. Attacking strongly, he soon found himself facing a fearsome counterattack, and errors under pressure forced his resignation on move 42; after a decade, Karpov's reign as world champion was over.

His battles for the title were far from over, however. The following year, 1986, saw the defeated champion granted a rematch, to compensate him for the fact that he had been leading the original, abandoned contest. Though Karpov was seemingly down and out after 16 games, three points behind, three wins in a row suddenly levelled the scores and offered hope of an unlikely victory, before Kasparov won one more game and drew the rest to retain his title 12½–11½. A fourth match between the pair took place in 1987, after Karpov was given a bye to the Candidates final (having been occupied playing Kasparov for almost the entire qualifying cycle); this time Karpov won the penultimate game to lead 12–11 with one game remaining: just a draw would see him regain his title. What followed, though, was a defeat; the 12–12 tie saw Kasparov retain his title and Karpov fall agonisingly short once more. Three years later, the same two players would meet for the world championship for a fifth and final time, and once again it was close, Kasparov prevailing 12½–11½.

Karpov would regain a version of the title in 1993 when Kasparov and his challenger Nigel Short decided to hold their

own contest outside the auspices of the official championship. Defeating Jan Timman to claim the vacant championship, he then retained it twice in 1996 and 1998, in matches against Gata Kamsky and Viswanathan Anand. The following year, however, when the authorities decided that the champion should defend his title as a contestant in a knock-out tournament rather than against a single challenger, Karpov, like Fischer before him, refused to take part.

Undisputed world champion for a decade, champion of a sort for six more years, and one half of one of the game's historic rivalries, Anatoly Karpov remains one of the greatest players of all time. Though his careful, positional style of play may have lacked the showy brilliance exhibited by both his predecessor and his successor, it nevertheless made him a fearsome opponent. Aged 73, he now serves as a politician in the Russian parliament.

KARPOV 1 KORCHNOI 0

BAGUIO (PHILIPPINES), 1978

Anatoly Karpov entered the 32nd match of his first world championship defence against Viktor Korchnoi in something of a crisis. Four games earlier, he had held a convincing lead, ahead by five wins to two and needing only one more victory to retain the title he had won from Bobby Fischer by default three years earlier. Now, suddenly, after three defeats in four games, he was as close to losing his title as he was to retaining it; with five wins apiece, one more defeat would see Korchnoi capture his crown. The pressure was on.

Karpov, as White, opened with 1 e4, and his opponent played the Pirc. After 10 moves, Korchnoi moved his Knight to the side of the board and then immediately back again, suggesting either indecisiveness or the lack of a plan; either way, he wasted two moves. As White dominated in the centre of the board, gathering his pieces for a King's side attack, his opponent prepared for his own attack down the open a-file. When Korchnoi moved his Queen to a8 to support his Rook on a4, Karpov pounced, advancing his e-Pawn to break open the centre and launch a powerful attack on both sides of the board at once. With Black's Queen trapped in the corner as his pieces regrouped to defend the threatened King's side attack, White won a Queen's side Pawn to leave him with two unopposed Pawns on that side of the board and a still-promising attack on the King's side. The game was adjourned on move 41, with White's b-Pawn marching relentlessly towards its Queening square, and White poised to break through decisively onto the seventh rank with his Queen. Korchnoi resigned the game without resuming, and Karpov – despite his wobble – had retained his title.

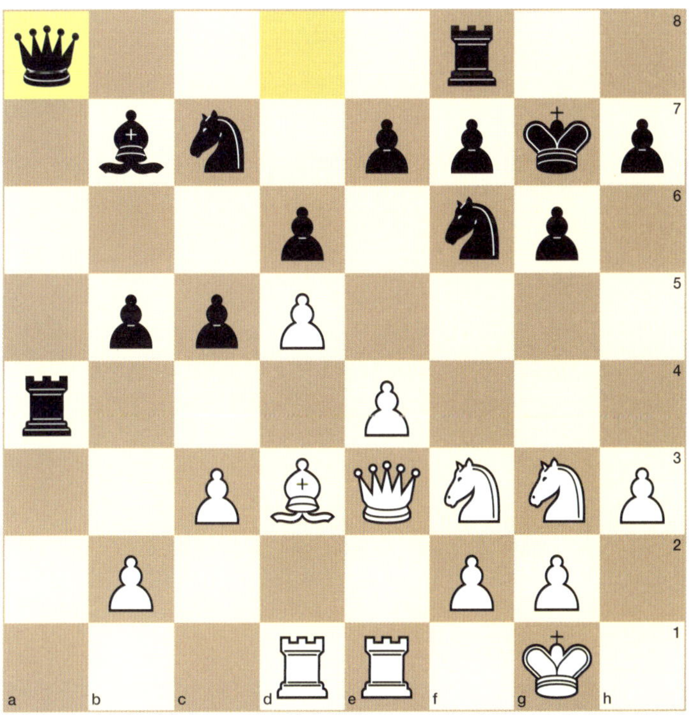

After Korchnoi played 24 … Qa8, Karpov advanced his Pawn to e5, opening the centre for his strongly placed pieces.

Garry Kasparov was ranked the world's strongest player for more than 20 years.

GARRY KASPAROV

(BORN 1963)

The 13th world chess champion was born Garik Kimovich Weinstein in 1963 to a Jewish father and an Armenian mother in Baku – now the capital of Azerbaijan, but at the time part of the Soviet Union. His father died when he was seven, and at 12 he adopted his mother's surname, Kasparov. Showing early promise at chess, the young Garry – named after U.S. President Harry Truman – began attending former champion Mikhail Botvinnik's chess school aged 10. In 1976, at the age of 13, he won the Soviet Junior Championship, held that year in Tbilisi, and repeated the feat the following year, winning eight of his nine games and drawing the other. Qualifying for the full Soviet Chess Championship in 1978 by winning a 64-player qualifying tournament, Kasparov took part in his first international competition in 1979 in Banja Luka, then part of Yugoslavia. The only unrated player in a field almost entirely comprised of Grandmasters, including the former world champion Tigran Petrosian, the 16-year-old nevertheless won the tournament undefeated, two points clear of his more established competitors. This stunning result was followed in 1980 by victory in the World Junior Chess Championship in Dortmund, and in 1981 by a tie for first place in the Soviet Chess Championship.

Aged just 19, Kasparov now found himself participating in the qualification process to find a challenger for world champion Anatoly Karpov. Winning the Moscow Interzonal tournament convincingly, the only player to remain undefeated over 13 rounds, Kasparov qualified for the Candidates Tournament, the youngest player to do so since Bobby Fischer in 1958. By now he was the world's number two in the official rankings, behind

only Karpov, and before the tournament cycle was complete, he would supplant the world champion to become the youngest top-ranked player of all time. Kasparov had little trouble winning the Candidates Tournament, losing only two games over three matches, defeating his fellow Soviet Alexander Beliavsky in the quarter-final, the two-time championship challenger Viktor Korchnoi in the semi-final, and former world champion Vasily Smyslov in the final. Now 21, and the top-ranked player in the world, he would challenge Anatoly Karpov for his crown.

The record five championship matches between Karpov and Kasparov from 1984 to 1990 were covered at length in the previous section: how Kasparov began the 1984 match disastrously with four defeats in the first nine games but had recovered to narrow the deficit to 5–3 before the marathon match was controversially halted; how he won the second match 13–11 to become, aged 22, the youngest world champion ever; how three defeats in a row in the third match almost cost Kasparov his title, before a late rally saw him win by one point; how only a victory in the final game of the fourth match saved him from relinquishing his title; and how the final contest between these two great rivals resulted in another single-point victory for the champion.

At the end of this long series of matches – 144 games over seven years, across five countries – Garry Kasparov was, aged 27, already a four-time world champion; his sixth title match would be very different from all that had come before. Unexpectedly, Karpov had lost in the semi-finals to the British player Nigel Short, who then went on to defeat the Dutchman Jan Timman in the final: for the first time, Kasparov would play someone other than Karpov for the title. Before the match could be played, however, Kasparov and Short announced that they would play their match not under the auspices of FIDE (the International

Kasparov was only 22 when he became world chess champion.

Between 1984 and 1990, Kasparov played five world championship matches against Anatoly Karpov.

Chess Federation), the organization that ran world chess, and which had organized the world championship since 1946, but instead under the flag of the newly formed Professional Chess Association, established by themselves. The split was the result of several factors, most notably that relations between Kasparov and FIDE's president had been strained ever since the abandonment of his first match against Karpov, and that the location for the match – originally Manchester – had been announced by FIDE without consulting the players.

The match itself, which took place in London, was something of a non-event: Kasparov won three of the first four games, and five of the first nine; after 20 games, he had retained his title by a margin of 12½–7½. Two years later, in 1995, he played his seventh title match, again under the auspices of the PCA, this time against the Indian Viswanathan Anand; after eight draws, Kasparov lost the first decisive game before four wins in the next five saw him prevail 10½–7½. The collapse of the PCA in 1996 left Kasparov unable to organize a series of qualification matches to find a challenger for his title, and after several failed attempts to set up matches with Anand and then Alexei Shirov, he finally played Vladimir Kramnik in October 2000, and relinquished his crown without winning a game, losing twice and drawing 13 games for a final score of 8½–6½. Though he was still ranked the number one player in the world – a position he held for a record 21 years – he was no longer world champion, and various attempts over the next few years to organize a challenge against various FIDE champions proved unsuccessful; in 2005 he announced his retirement from competitive chess, shortly after winning a record ninth victory in the historic annual Linares tournament.

Kasparov's exciting attacking style, influenced by Alekhine, Fischer, and Tal, made him a striking contrast to his predecessor

as world champion, the more positional Anatoly Karpov. He was one of the first players to make extensive use of chess computers for game analysis, and even played several matches against the leading computers of his time, famously losing a six-game match against Deep Blue in 1997. Since retiring from competitive chess, he has been an active political force in opposition to the Russian government of Vladimir Putin, unsuccessfully attempting to stand for Russian president in 2007, and opposing the regime from abroad since going into exile in 2013.

KARPOV 0 KASPAROV 1
MOSCOW, 1985

After 15 games of their second world championship match, Karpov and Kasparov were tied at two wins apiece. The initiative had swung from side to side, with first the challenger and then the champion taking the lead, but with nine games left, five of them with White, Karpov needed only to match his opponent point for point to retain his title. For Kasparov to wrest it from him, he would need to do something decisive.

Game 16 began identically to game 12 – a Sicilian Defence in which Black offers White a Pawn in return for a positional advantage. That game had finished in an easy draw for Black, but Karpov, playing White, had had a week to find an improvement and on move 11 he played it, advancing his King's Bishop one square rather than three. Kasparov's immediate response, also pre-prepared, was to advance his own Bishop to a strong attacking square (11 … Bc5). It was a move that displayed his attacking intent, even though post-match analysis would find it flawed since, with best play,

White can hold on to the extra Pawn without too much risk. By move 16, Black had in return for his Pawn a Knight on d3, deep within White's position: the 'Octopus' Knight, as it would become known. It would stay there for 18 moves, exerting such control over the game that White would eventually only remove it at the cost of his Queen. Though White gained two Knights and a Bishop for that Queen, his position was by this point so poor that Karpov resigned after Black's 40th move. Kasparov had achieved the win he needed and, with it, the initiative. He would win again in game 19, to put him – aged just 22 – on the verge of becoming world champion.

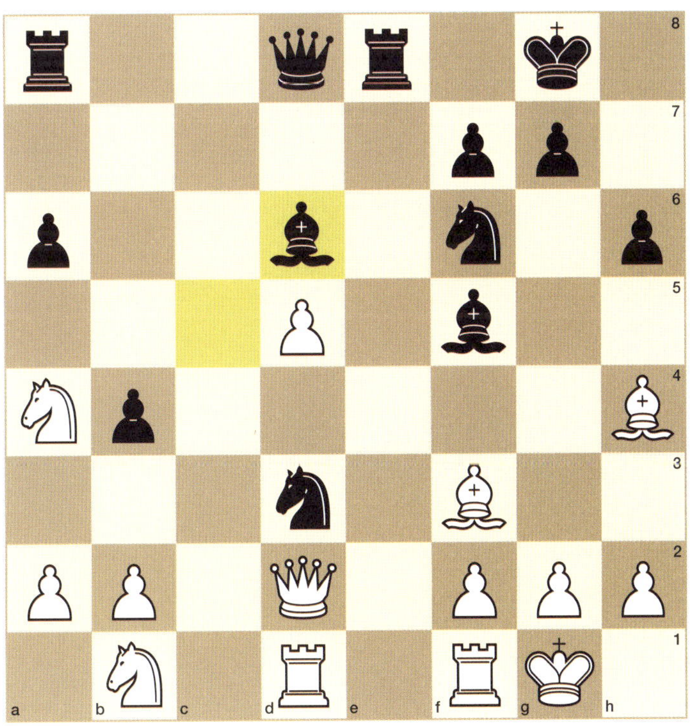

Position after 19 ... Bd6, with Kasparov's 'Octopus' Knight dominating White's position.

Judit Polgár is widely regarded as the greatest female player of all time.

JUDIT POLGÁR

(BORN 1976)

The greatest female player of all time never won the women's world championship, though her older sister did. Refusing to compete in women-only tournaments from the age of 14, Judit Polgár spent more than 20 years playing against some of the greatest male players of all time – and often beat them. On her retirement from the game in 2014, aged 38, she held – or had previously held – all manner of records: at the age of 15, she had become the world's youngest ever Grandmaster, a record she captured from the legendary Bobby Fischer; in 2005 she became the first – and so far only – woman to compete in the later stages of the world championship cycle; and she remains the only woman ever to be ranked within the world's top 10, as well as the only woman ever to have defeated the reigning world number one. Ranked women's number one for 25 years, Judit Polgár rightly deserves her place in any list of the game's most remarkable players.

She was born in 1976 in Budapest to Hungarian-Jewish parents who raised her – and her two older sisters, Zsuzsa and Zsofia – to be chess prodigies. Convinced that geniuses were born, not made, László and Klára Polgár educated their daughters at home, employing professional players to coach them. Zsuzsa, the eldest child, became the world's top-rated female player in 1986, aged 15; 10 years later, she would become women's world champion, defeating Xie Jun of China. Zsofia, two years younger, would reach the rank of International Master and finish second in the World Junior Championships in 1994, before abandoning the game. But Judit would go on to surpass all her sisters' achievements. By the age of six,

she was already playing in tournaments, earning her International Master title at 12; by the time she was 13, she was already ranked among the world's top hundred players of any gender. Her final women-only tournament was the 1990 Women's Olympiad – the international team tournament – where she and her sisters helped Hungary to win the gold medal.

Winning the Hungarian National Championship in 1991 saw Judit Polgár become the youngest ever Grandmaster, and only the fourth woman to achieve the title, after Nona Gaprindashvili, Maia Chiburdanidze, and her own sister Zsuzsa. The following year, she finished second in the historic Linares tournament, behind former world champion Anatoly Karpov; then in 1993, after sharing victory at Hastings with the Russian Grandmaster Yevgeny Bareev, she played another former world champion, Boris Spassky, in a 10-game match, winning 5½–4½. The same year she became the first woman to qualify for the Interzonal stage of the FIDE World Championship qualifying cycle, missing out on qualification for the Candidates Tournament by half a point. At the rival PCA tournament, she also finished a half point outside the qualification spots.

More tournament successes followed and by 1996, aged only 19, Polgár was ranked in the top 10 players in the world, competing regularly against the world's strongest players. In 1998, she scored two notable successes, defeating Karpov 5–3 in a match played to a 30-minute time limit, and sharing the U.S. Open title with the Soviet-American Grandmaster Boris Gulko. Over the next 16 years, Polgár would play on equal terms with players of the calibre of Karpov and Kasparov, Anand and Timman, achieving some stunning results, including reaching the final eight of the 2011 Chess World Cup, defeating en route

Judit Polgár (centre) with her sisters Zsuzsa (left) and Zsofia (right).

In 1993, Polgár defeated former world champion Boris Spassky in a 10-game match.

the number one seed and world number five Sergey Karjakin. Twice she reached the later stages of the world championship contest: in 2005, she competed in an eight-player tournament to decide the new FIDE world champion but finished last, with just a single win from 14 games; two years later, she would be eliminated in the first round of qualifying for the equivalent tournament.

A highly tactical player, Judit Polgár typically played aggressive opening variations and was particularly strong at games played to faster time limits. Like Emanuel Lasker, she would often tailor her style to a particular opponent, aiming to disconcert her adversary by targeting their weaknesses. As the world's strongest female player, Polgár seemed to prompt a curious hostility from her male counterpart, Garry

Kasparov. Back in 1990, when she was only 13, the world champion had suggested to a reporter that, thanks to the 'imperfections of the feminine psyche', Polgár would never be a 'great grand master'. When the pair played four years later, at the 1994 Linares tournament, Kasparov changed his mind about a move moments after letting go of the piece – an unacceptable action at any level of the game – but no action was taken by the authorities; Polgár confronted the champion about it after the game, only for him to tell an interviewer later that 'a girl her age' – she was now 17 – 'should be taught some good manners'. It would be seven years before Polgár would draw a game with Kasparov – twice at the Linares tournament in 2001 – and a further year before she would defeat him, as part of a match between Russia and the Rest of the World, played to a half-hour time limit. Using an opening variation Kasparov had played himself quite recently, Polgár launched an attack on his King which left him no option but to resign. After almost a decade, she had got her revenge.

Since retiring from competitive play in 2014, Polgár has used her status as the greatest female player of all time to encourage others to play chess, and to advocate the use of chess for educational purposes. The Judit Polgár Chess Foundation, founded in 2012, promotes chess in Hungary and globally, encouraging children to play the game and training teachers to use it as a means of developing learners' problem solving and strategic thinking skills. An annual Judit Polgár Chess Festival, organized by the Foundation, combines tournaments and family activities with an educational conference. Having grown up with chess at the heart of her education, Polgár is determined that others too should learn its benefits.

SHIROV 0 POLGÁR 1
BUENOS AIRES, 1994

The 1994 Buenos Aires Tournament was something of an oddity. Organized to celebrate the 60th birthday of the Soviet Grandmaster Lev Polugaevsky, an expert in the Sicilian Defence, it had the unusual stipulation that every game should, in his honour, start with the Open Sicilian (1 e4 c5 2 Nf3 e6/d6/Nc6 3 d4 cxd4 4 Nxd4). Among the eight players taking part were former world champion Anatoly Karpov, future world champion Viswanathan Anand, current world number two Alexei Shirov, and the 18-year-old women's number one, Judit Polgár. It would be won by the Russian Valery Salov, a late replacement for Polugaevsky, who was too unwell to play in his own tournament.

Polgár, who would finish joint third, had won her first game against Shirov, with White, but it was her second that caught the attention. In line with the tournament rules, she played the Taimanov variation of the Sicilian (2 … e6, 4 … Nc6) and Shirov replied with an aggressive advance of his King's side Pawns to leave him with a line of three Pawns on e4, f4, and g4. Polgár's response was remarkable. Advancing her own g-Pawn, she offered her opponent a Pawn advantage in return for King's side weaknesses that she could exploit with her Knights.

Within a few moves, both Knights were occupying key squares on that side and White's King was so boxed in by his own pieces that a rare checkmate by Black's two Knights was a real possibility.

Polgár offered her Queen in the knowledge that a fork from her one of her powerful Knights would win it back immediately, but Shirov didn't take the bait. His only way out was to give up Rook for Bishop, but even this was not enough to save him, and he resigned after Black's 29th move. The game became known as 'Polgár's Immortal'.

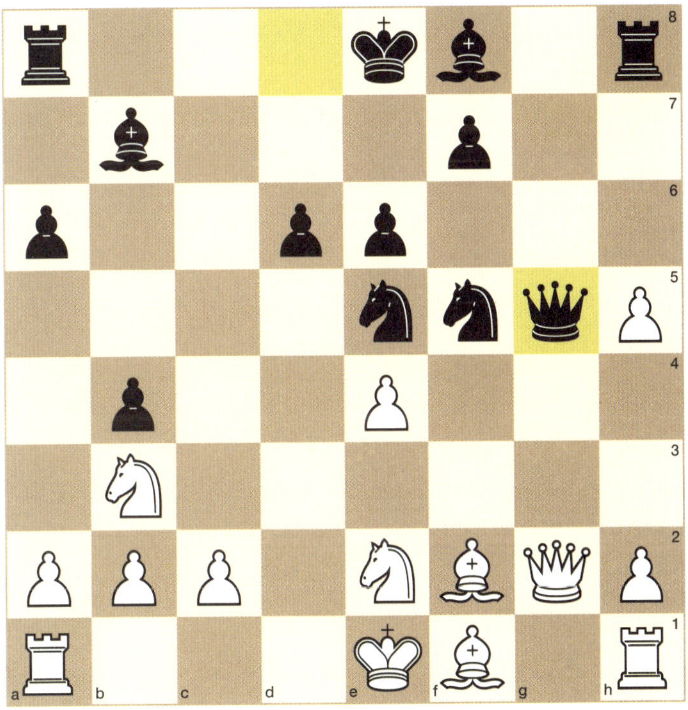

With 15 … Qxg5, Black offers up her Queen; if White accepts the sacrifice with 16 Qxg5, Black wins it back immediately with 16 … Nf3 and has a Pawn advantage.

The Norwegian Magnus Carlsen lost only two games across five world championship matches.

MAGNUS CARLSEN

(BORN 1990)

When Magnus Carlsen resigned his world title in July 2022, he did so as an undefeated five-times champion who had held that title for almost nine years. In those five championship matches, he had lost only two games out of 63; he had achieved the highest rating in history, outstripping even Garry Kasparov, and he had been world number one for more than a decade. By any reckoning, he was already one of history's greatest players, as outstanding at the quicker forms of chess as he was at the classical version: within months of his announcement, he had won a fourth rapid chess championship, where players typically have less than half an hour to play all their moves, and a fifth world blitz championship, where the time limit is three minutes, plus an additional two seconds following each move. He retained both titles the following year.

Born in Tønsberg, Norway, in November 1990, Carlsen showed an aptitude for intellectual puzzles from a remarkably young age: he was solving jigsaw puzzles by the age of two, and later graduated to memorizing the locations, flags, and capitals of all the countries in the world. His father taught him chess at the age of five and the young boy was soon spending much of his time playing games by himself. He entered his first tournament in 1999, aged eight, and played almost 300 official games over the next three years, tying for first place in the world under-12 championship and achieving the rank of International Master. On leaving primary school in 2003, he took a year off school to play in European tournaments, finishing ninth in the world under-14 championship and earning the Grandmaster title the following year, aged only 13. The next few years would see a series of tournament triumphs and broken records as the teenage prodigy rapidly became one of the top-ranked

Carlsen defeated Viswanathan Anand in 2013 to become world champion.

players in the world. At 17, he qualified for the world championship Candidates Tournament, but lost in the first round to the Armenian Levon Aronian; in January 2010, aged 19, he became the youngest player ever to be ranked world number one.

Carlsen first seriously challenged for the world championship title in 2013. Though he had qualified for the eight-player Candidates stage of the previous cycle, a series of knock-out matches designed to find a challenger for title-holder Viswanathan Anand, Carlsen had withdrawn before the contest began, stating in a letter to the organizers that he didn't find the system 'sufficiently modern and fair' to motivate him to participate. With the previous match system replaced by a single eight-player tournament for 2013, Carlsen entered the final round level on points with the Russian former champion Vladimir Kramnik but leading on tie-break scores: a win in his final match, with White, would guarantee him victory and the right to challenge Anand for his title. Pushing hard for that win in a level position, Carlsen got into serious time trouble and lost, but when Kramnik lost his game as well, the Norwegian's tie-break score was enough to see him through; a match with Anand awaited. The match took place in Chennai that November: 12 games played to classical time limits, with faster games to function as a tie-break if scores were level after that. After four initial draws, Carlsen won two games in a row to lead 4–2 at the halfway point; one more win and three more draws in the next four games saw him crowned world champion with two games to spare, 6½–3½. A year later, Carlsen played his second title match, again against Anand, who had won the Candidates Tournament to win the right to challenge for the title he had lost the previous year. This time the match was a little less one-sided, with Anand winning one game, but three wins for Carlsen saw him retain his title with a game to spare, 6½–4½.

Carlsen's third world championship match, in 2016, was a much closer affair. This time, his challenger was Sergey Karjakin, born in Ukraine but a Russian citizen since 2009. All but two of the initial 12 games were drawn, Karjakin winning the eighth and Carlsen the 10th; four games at faster speeds were thus employed as a tie-break and, after two more draws, the Norwegian won games 15 and 16 to retain his title. Two years later, Carlsen was once again taken to a tie-break in defence of his title by the American challenger Fabiano Caruana: all 12 of their regular games were drawn – the first time this had ever happened in a world championship match – but again the champion prevailed at faster limits, winning three rapid games in a row to retain his title.

Carlsen's fifth and final title match took place in Dubai in 2021, against the Russian Ian Nepomniachtchi. After the two previous matches had required tie-breaks, the number of games for this contest was increased from 12 to 14, but in the event only 11 were needed: after five closely fought draws, the sixth game lasted eight hours and a record 136 moves before a mistake from Nepomniachtchi in a tough position allowed Carlsen, who had a Rook, Knight, and two Pawns against the Russian's Queen, to win. After this, the challenger's play declined, and errors in three of the next five games gave Carlsen victory – and a fifth world title – by a four-point margin with three games left to play. Within

four days of his triumph, however, the Norwegian announced that he was no longer as motivated as he once had been by the challenge of defending his title, and that he might only participate in a further championship match if the fast-rising Alireza Firouzja were his opponent. A year later, with the challenger confirmed as Ian Nepomniachtchi – Firouzja had finished a disappointing sixth in the Candidates Tournament – Carlsen confirmed that he would not take part. After nine years, and four successful title defences, he would retire undefeated, moving away from classical chess, where he felt opening preparation had become overly dominant, towards the blitz and rapid tournaments at which he continued to excel.

ANAND 0 CARLSEN 1

CHENNAI, 2013

By game nine of his 2013 world championship match against Viswanathan Anand, the challenger Magnus Carlsen was already on the brink of victory. Wins in games five and six of the 12-game series had left him needing just three more draws – or a win and a draw – from the four remaining games. His opponent needed at least two wins, making this – Anand's penultimate game as White – a must-win game for him. What resulted was one of the more remarkable games in world championship history, with three Queens on the board at once, a seemingly irresistible mating attack, and a final blunder that left the result of the game – and the match – beyond doubt.

Having played 1 e4 in his previous four games as White, none of which he had won, Anand switched to 1 d4 and played a sharp variation against Black's Nimzo-Indian Defence. Carlsen's response was to avoid the well-known options and then raise the stakes by castling King's side into the face of his opponent's attack. As White's Pawns advanced on the King's side, so Black's did the same on the Queen's side, so that by move 22, White had Pawns on e5, f5, and g5, while Black had a passed Pawn on b3 just two moves away from Queening. White then advanced his f-Pawn, compelling Black to create a hole in his defence that opened up possibilities for checkmate from White's Queen on g7 or h7. But before Anand could quite get his pieces in place for the final attack, Carlsen's b-Pawn had reached the final rank and Queened with check. Had Anand found the right response – interposing his Bishop instead of his Knight – then Carlsen would have had to give up his new Queen almost immediately to escape a mating attack; instead, the champion's blunder left him no option but to resign.

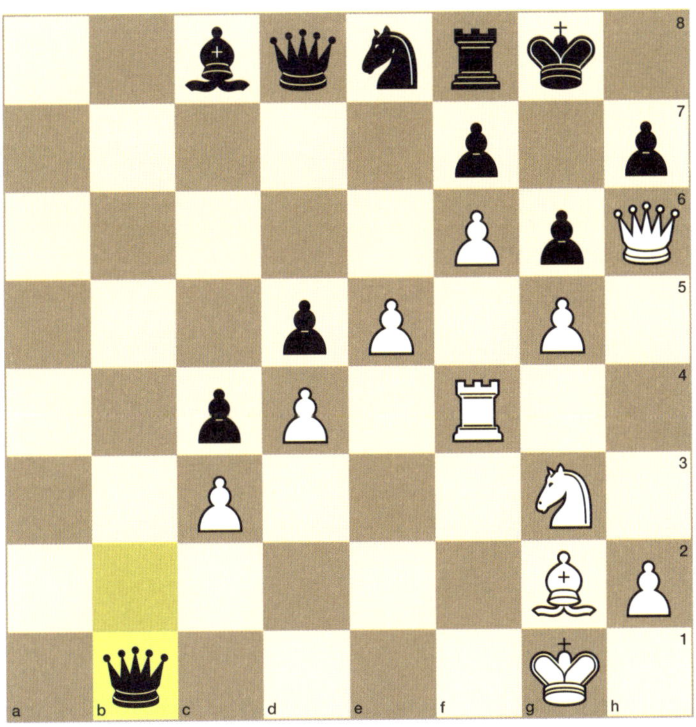

After Carlsen's 27 … b1=Q+, Anand blundered by blocking the check with his Knight rather than his Bishop and resigned a move later.

PICTURE CREDITS

Alamy: 8 (Pictorial Press), 13 (Zoonar), 15 (Heritage Image Partnership), 17 (Granger Historical Picture Archive), 18 (Florilegius), 19 (Granger Historical Picture Archive), 24 (Album), 27 (Associated Press), 29 (Abbus Archive), 32 (BFA), 34 (Chronicle), 42 (Ian Dagnall), 44 bottom (Chronicle), 56 (PA Images), 58 top (Still Gravity), 66 top (Ian Shipley TYS), 92 (Alex MacNaughton), 94 (Sueddeutsche Zeitung), 106 (Album), 118 (Penta Springs), 124 (CSU Archives / Everett Collection), 128 (Keystone Press), 134 (Associated Press), 138 (Universal Images Group), 141 (Associated Press), 154 (Zuma Press), 156 (Associated Press)

Cleveland Museum of Art: 10

Dreamstime: 58 bottom & 60 bottom (Stefan Hermans), 68 (Wirestock)

From the Collection of Frank Camaratta, ChessAntiques.com: 40, 41, 48 both, 50 both, 52 top, 53-55, 62 bottom, 64 bottom, 66 bottom

From the House of Staunton, HouseOfStaunton.com: 51

Getty Images: 16 (DeAgostini), 30 (Pictures from History / Universal Images Group), 35 (Oscar Gustav Rejlander / Hulton Archive), 37 (Bongarts), 38 (Alain Bachellier), 43 (Photo 12), 46 bottom (Bettmann), 70 (Pierre-Philippe Marcou / AFP), 109 (Keystone-France), 112 (Hulton-Deutsch Collection / Corbis), 114 (Keystone-France), 120 (Dennis Oulds / Central Press), 126 (Bettmann), 132 (Universal History Archive), 142 (Miroslav Zajic), 146 & 149 (Yvonne Hemsey), 150 (Attila Kisbenedek / AFP)

iStock: 21 (ZU_09)

Library of Congress: 22, 100

Metropolitan Museum of Art, New York: 6, 12, 60 top, 62 top, 64 top

Public domain: 11, 28, 52 bottom

Shutterstock: 49 (Andrew Matt)

Staunton Castle, StauntonCastle.com: 44 top, 45, 46 top, 47

BIBLIOGRAPHY

Harold C. Schonberg, *Grandmasters of Chess* (London: David-Poynter, 1974)

William Hartston, *The Kings of Chess* (London: Pavilion, 1985)